OVERCOMING ANXIETY

A REFLECTIVE GUIDE FOR ADULTS TO BREAK THE
CYCLE OF WORRY AND TAKE CONTROL OF
YOUR MIND

KIRK TEACHOUT

CONTENTS

INTRODUCTION

You know the feeling. You're working hard at the office or cooking dinner for your family, just minding your own business, when all of a sudden your heart starts beating in your throat. Your hands clam up — they're shaking — and you're not sure why. You try to take a deep breath to calm yourself down, but the tightness in your chest only seems to get worse. "What is happening to me?" You wonder out loud. "*Why* is this happening to me?"

Did you know that anxiety is the most common mental illness there is? Around 30% of U.S. adults will experience some sort of anxiety-related disorder at some point in their lives. If you've been struggling or have ever struggled with an anxiety disorder, you're definitely not alone. Millions of people all over the world

— including myself — have been there before. Anxiety is brutal, and there's no "quick fix" for it, but if you're willing to put the work in, it's absolutely possible for you to take back your life.

Take my good friend, Charles, for example. Charles is one of the kindest people I've ever met, but he's unfortunately struggled with anxiety for most of his life. Before he learned how to overcome his anxiety, it was a heavy burden that he carried around with him every single day. I could see how it affected him, both mentally and physically. He often had trouble eating and sleeping, and when we attended social events, he would bite his fingernails and wring his hands — both of which were anxious habits.

Charles knew he needed help, but he had no idea where to look. Anxiety had been plaguing him for years, and over time, he'd tried many different coping mechanisms, some of which weren't particularly healthy. He felt like he was drowning in his worries, and it was getting more and more difficult for him to keep his head above the surface.

When he thought all hope was lost, Charles happened to stumble upon the solution to his problem. It was as if a light bulb had gone off in his head. *This is it!* He thought to himself. *I'm going to be okay!* Finally, he had a clear path laid out in front of him, and following this path would eventually allow him to overcome his anxiety. Charles knew it wouldn't be easy, but he took it one step at a time, and slowly but surely began to see improvements.

Charles realized that the key to overcoming his anxiety was to confront it head-on. He recognized that he had to identify the root causes of his worries if he was going to successfully confront them, and from there came up with practical ways to manage his anxiety triggers. He learned how to prioritize self-care and began exercising regularly. He ate a healthy diet, and practiced mindful meditation, which helped to calm his mind.

Of course, the changes weren't immediate. Charles didn't walk the path of recovery without tripping over tree roots every now and then. He kept at it, though, and eventually, his anxiety began to subside. The world around him began to look a little brighter. He could finally breathe a little easier, and was able to do things his anxiety had previously prevented him from doing.

It can be hard to know where to turn or what to do when you're dealing with anxiety, but the solution to your problem may be closer than you think. By taking small steps every day and being persistent — just like Charles was — you can learn how to manage your anxiety and live a happier, healthier life. You have the power to overcome your worries. It all starts with taking that first step.

There are a lot of things that could be making you anxious in your everyday life. The world is turbulent, and times are tough. You might be dealing with the anxiety that comes with growing up and moving out of your parents' house, or perhaps you've been run ragged by the corporate rat race and dread going to work every morning. At times, you might find yourself getting anxious for no identifiable reason. Your brain is seemingly getting hyperstimulated by something, but you're not sure what.

Anxiety mainly affects people between the ages of 18 to 29 and 30 to 44 (although, people of all ages can experience it). Millennials and Gen Z adults are significantly more anxious than previous generations, and women in particular are twice as likely to be diagnosed with an anxiety disorder. This has a lot to do with significant societal changes that have taken place. Millennials were forced to take menial jobs in 2008 when the Great Recession hit, and Gen Z adults were forced to put important milestones on hold when the Covid-19 pandemic wreaked havoc in 2020.

Women are more likely to experience anxiety than men due to a number of factors, such as hormone fluctuations, brain chemistry, sexism in the workplace, objectification, or domestic violence in relationships. Existing as a woman is, in general, more anxiety-inducing than existing as a man. My female friends have told me about the fear they experience while walking alone at night, which is something I've never had to worry about as a man.

They've shared stories about being harassed on public transportation, and being objectified at work. They deal with these things every day, and they somehow manage to turn the other cheek (or retaliate if it's safe to do so) and go about their lives. I admire their strength, but it's sad that these issues have become normalized. I'm not saying these things never happen to men — they do — but there's no denying that women are more likely to experience things like street harassment and objectification. It makes perfect sense that they're more anxious.

Anxiety is on the rise, and it has been for several years. Why, you might ask? Life in the U.S. has gotten more stressful for sure, but it's important to note that people may be more inclined to report their feelings of anxiety in this day and age. Mental health issues have become less stigmatized and better understood by the masses, so young people in particular will be more likely to admit when they're feeling anxious or depressed.

It's also important to keep in mind that simply experiencing anxious feelings does not equate to having an anxiety disorder. Everyone feels anxious sometimes, but those with Generalized Anxiety Disorder (GAD) will oftentimes experience anxiety that extends beyond logic and reason. For a person with GAD, the smallest stressor or inconvenience can feel like the end of the world.

If you feel as if you're in a constant state of distress or panic — like you've always got something biting at the back of your mind — I see you. If you get anxious about being anxious, just know that you're not alone. You might feel like your anxiety has been getting in the way of your relationships, as well as preventing you from forming new relationships with people you're interested in romantically or otherwise.

Perhaps your anxiety has started to significantly impact your sleeping and eating habits, meaning it has not only taken a toll on your mental health, but on your physical health as well. As with physical ailments that go untreated, mental ailments have a tendency to get worse over time, especially if you don't know what steps to take in order to help yourself. If you're tired of being at the mercy of your anxiety — if the panic attacks and sleepless nights have gotten to be too much — you're in the right place.

In this book, I'll be sharing the knowledge I've gathered over several years in hopes that it will provide you with the tools you need to confront your anxiety head-on. We'll be going over the symptoms of anxiety, as well as some common triggers and life changes that may have caused you to feel anxious in the past (and, retroactively, the future). I don't claim to have all the answers, and there aren't any "quick fixes" I can recommend. However, I can guarantee that you'll have a full tool belt by the time you reach the end of this book.

Like my friend, Charles, you can learn how to cope with your anxiety and live the life you were always meant to live. It won't be easy and it might take some time, but with enough persistence and determination, you'll get there. So, without further ado, let's get into what it takes to overcome anxiety.

1

ANXIETY: FROM A TO WHY

> "*Whatever is going to happen will happen, whether we worry or not.*"
>
> — ANA MONNAR

Anxiety is a beast with many faces. Think Koh The Face Stealer from the spirit world in the popular animated cartoon, *Avatar: The Last Airbender*. The multifaceted nature of anxiety can lead people to believe they're not actually experiencing it — even when they very much are. Anxiety can look how you might expect it to look (i.e. your mother pacing around the house and running her fingers through her hair while engaging in a stressful phone call), or it might hide itself within certain characteristics, such as perfectionism or obsession over minute details.

Sometimes, it can be difficult to differentiate between generalized anxiety and the feeling of simply being anxious. When my anxiety was at its worst, I tried absolutely everything to ignore it, assuming I was just anxious because of work or upcoming life events. I eventually realized, however, that it's not normal to dread going to work every day. You might feel slightly annoyed that you have to go to work some days, but I was losing sleep and vomiting every other morning due to my dread and anxiety surrounding work.

My job wasn't even particularly stressful at the time. I just dreaded it for *some* reason, despite the fact I actually sort of enjoyed it in the moment. This is just one example of how anxiety can make you think illogically and irrationally. If you've ever felt sick with worry before doing something you've done a million times before, or if you've ever said "no" to going out with your friends because the thought of being social made you anxious, you know what I'm talking about.

Whether you're aware of it or not, your anxiety is preventing you from living your life to the fullest. It masquerades as something that's keeping you safe, but in reality, anxiety is like an overprotective parent or partner. It's so focused on "keeping you safe" that it's actually preventing you from enjoying the things you used to enjoy. It's like in Disney's *Tangled*, when Mother Gothel tells Rapunzel that she must stay locked up in the tower "for her own safety." Rapunzel, with a little help, realizes that this isn't the case. She eventually leaves the tower and faces her fears — and you can too.

WHAT IS ANXIETY?

Anxiety is a sensation that's often accompanied by tense feelings, worried thoughts, and bodily changes such as elevated blood pressure and an increased heart rate. People with anxiety disorders like Generalized Anxiety Disorder (GAD) and Obsessive Compulsive Disorder (OCD) are typically plagued by intrusive thoughts or recurring worries. They might stay away from specific situations (i.e. going out to dinner with their friends or asking for a promotion at work) out of fear. They might also experience bodily side effects like sweating, trembling, nausea, and vomiting.

Although they're not the same thing, fear and anxiety are often used indiscriminately. It's important that you're able to differentiate between the two, however. To put it simply, fear is a proper, in-the-moment reaction to a clearly recognizable and specific danger, whereas anxiety is a long-lasting, widely focused, future-oriented response to a vague threat.

What Causes Anxiety?

It's normal to occasionally feel anxious, especially in stressful situations. If you experience intense, excessive, and constant concern in ordinary situations, however, you may want to get evaluated for an anxiety disorder. Anxiety disorders usually involve recurrent bouts of extreme worry or panic that can peak in a matter of minutes. This is known as a "panic attack." It's important to note that not everyone with an anxiety disorder experiences panic attacks and not everyone who experiences panic attacks has an anxiety disorder by default.

These uncomfortable, hard-to-control, prolonged feelings of anxiety may impede your everyday activities and affect your personal relationships. Childhood or adolescence may be the first time symptoms appear, and oftentimes, these symptoms will last well into adulthood. The causes of anxiety can vary significantly. Whether or not you develop an anxiety disorder depends on your genetics, your past trauma, your physical health, your brain chemistry, the environment you're in, and the prejudices you face as a result of your race, gender, or sexuality. We'll go over this in a bit more detail later, so stick around!

Risk Factors

As a human being, you've got to keep in mind that while you're strong, you're also delicate. Perhaps you've heard the Reza Farazmand quote: "Don't forget to drink water and get sunlight. You're basically a houseplant with more complicated emotions." Most human beings deal with an immense amount of stress throughout their daily lives, and some self-treat their stressed out feelings with drugs and/or alcohol. Let's briefly go over some of the risk factors — like drugs and alcohol — that are associated with anxiety. Again, we'll go over this in more detail later, so don't worry!

Trauma

Children who experienced neglect or witnessed upsetting events while growing up are more likely to eventually develop an anxiety-related disorder. Anxiety disorders can also manifest in adults who go through traumatic events.

Stress Buildup

Anxiety and various anxiety disorders can also be triggered by major life events (or smaller, stressful life events that have accumulated over time). It's like the steam that builds up in a pressure cooker. If that steam doesn't eventually get released, you're going to end up with rice all over your kitchen walls.

Stress Due to Illness

When you're experiencing a serious health problem, you may worry a lot about things like your future and your treatment. This is quite normal, but if you're sick with worry all the time due to being concerned or stressed out about your illness, it could be an indication of an underlying anxiety disorder.

Other Mental Health Disorders

Anxiety disorders — like OCD, for example — tend to go hand-in-hand with other mental health disorders, such as depression, PTSD, and ADHD. Your anxiety may intensify your other mental health issues, or vice versa.

Genetics

Anxiety disorders may run in your family. Sit down with your mom, dad, or grandparents, and ask them if they've ever struggled with an anxiety disorder. At least one of your family members probably did or does, in which case you can talk to them about your own experiences with anxiety (if they're open to that).

Drugs or Alcohol

Many people use drugs and/or alcohol because they feel like it relieves their anxiety. However, the fact of the matter is, misuse of drugs and alcohol will usually make your anxiety symptoms worse.

ANXIETY DISORDER... OR JUST ANXIOUS?

At this point, you might be wondering: what exactly is the difference between anxiety and an anxiety disorder? Anxiety is a typical response to a stressful event or circumstance. It's essentially your body's internal alarm system. It warns you about situations that it perceives as dangerous, and prepares your body to either fight back, retreat, or stay very still. This is commonly known as the "fight, flight, or freeze" response.

An occasional bout of anxiety can be quite beneficial. For instance, it might inspire you to complete an assignment at work or carry pepper spray when walking alone at night. Even joyful occasions, like moving to a new town, or marking a significant milestone in your career can trigger anxiety. This is partly a result of the adrenaline that gets released into your system when you go through a major life event.

Typical Anxiety

Typical, everyday anxiety is almost always a response to stress. Most people feel anxious before giving a presentation at work or going out on a date with someone they like for the first time. When the stressor is over (i.e. you give a great presentation or have a nice time on your date), the anxiety goes away.

Anxiety Disorders, However...

Those who suffer from anxiety disorders typically still feel anxious even *after* whatever has been causing them stress ends or is removed from the scenario. Oftentimes, people with anxiety disorders feel like they can't control their worrying, and some will even get physically ill if their anxiety becomes particularly severe.

There are essentially two things that define an anxiety disorder. First of all, your anxiety must be out of proportion to the situation or situations that are causing you stress. Second of all, if your anxiety makes it difficult for you to function normally, this could be an indication that you're suffering from an anxiety disorder. Basically, if your anxiety is so severe that it's negatively impacting your quality of life, it may be time to get a professional evaluation.

DIFFERENT TYPES OF ANXIETY DISORDERS

Anxiety disorders are quite common and treatable, but this does not mean they are easy to cope with. Experiencing an anxiety disorder can be quite confusing and disorienting. Those who aren't sure what they're experiencing might fall deeper into a state of panic, further exacerbating their anxious feelings. There are several different types of anxiety disorders you should be aware of. Simply being in the know can help you identify certain signs and symptoms before they get worse.

Generalized Anxiety Disorder (GAD)

Generalized Anxiety Disorder is one of the most commonly-experienced mental disorders in the world. It can alter your behavior as well as change the way you perceive the universe around you. Those with GAD typically experience restlessness, general unease, irritability, and self-doubt. Some GAD sufferers have trouble forming meaningful relationships and focusing on important tasks because their anxious feelings are holding them back.

Panic Disorder

The majority of the time, panic attacks start abruptly and without any sort of warning. If you have Panic Disorder, a panic attack may happen to you at any moment — whether you're driving, shopping, sleeping, or in the midst of an important conference call. You might experience panic episodes frequently or infrequently depending on several factors. Although there are many different types of panic attacks, symptoms (such as sweating, quivering, nausea, and an elevated heart rate) typically climax within a few minutes. After a panic attack, you might feel exhausted and emotionally drained.

Phobias

A person with a specific phobia will feel intense, irrational dread toward a certain circumstance, a living thing, a location, or a particular item. When someone has a phobia, they typically plan their lives around steering clear of things they perceive as risky. The imagined danger is always larger than the perceived threat that the fear-causing factor actually poses. Agoraphobia, for example, is a very common and irrational phobia.

For those who don't know, Agoraphobia is the fear of not being able to escape a certain situation or place. Examples include being away from home or being stuck in an airplane. Agoraphobia is frequently misinterpreted as the fear of wide open spaces, but it can also refer to being cooped up in a tiny area, like an elevator, or bus. Other common phobias include Claustrophobia (the fear of being in a confined space), Emetophobia (the fear of vomiting), and Arachnophobia (the fear of spiders).

Social Anxiety Disorder

Feeling shy or uneasy under specific circumstances is not always a symptom of Social Anxiety Disorder. Various personality traits and life events can affect a person's social comfort levels. Some people are inherently reserved and others are more outgoing (i.e. extroversion and introversion). The fear, anxiety, and avoidance that come with Social Anxiety Disorder are different from normal anxiety or uncertainty because they can affect relationships, routines, work, school, and hobbies. The onset of Social Anxiety Disorder usually occurs during the teenage years, although it can also happen in younger children and adults as well.

Separation Anxiety Disorder

It can be difficult for professionals to diagnose Separation Anxiety Disorder. Usually, a diagnosis can be made when the symptoms are excessive for the developmental stage that the person experiencing said symptoms is currently in. Separation Anxiety Disorder also tends to impair everyday functioning, unlike run-of-the-mill separation anxiety, which is not typically debilitating for most people who experience it.

The symptoms of Separation Anxiety Disorder may include extreme and ongoing anxiety about being away from home or loved ones, ongoing fear of losing a parent or another loved one due to sickness or disaster, and a constant fear of bad things happening, such as getting lost, abducted, or separated from your loved ones. Separation Anxiety Disorder typically stems from past trauma surrounding abandonment.

Post-Traumatic Stress Disorder (PTSD)

The first signs of Post-Traumatic Stress Disorder may emerge about one month after a traumatic incident takes place, however, some symptoms may take years to fully manifest. Oftentimes, the symptoms of PTSD (recurrent and unwanted distressing memories, night-mares, emotional turmoil, and avoidance of situations that are reminiscent of past trauma) can bring on significant issues in social, professional, and romantic interactions. Intrusive memories, avoidance, negative thought patterns, and changes in bodily and psychological responses are the four main categories professionals use to diagnose PTSD.

Acute Stress Disorder

Some people may experience Acute Stress Disorder in the days and weeks following a stressful event. Within a month of said event, Acute Stress Disorder might manifest in full (much like PTSD). It usually lasts for a minimum of three days or a maximum of one month. Acute Stress Disorder patients typically exhibit symptoms resembling those of Post-Traumatic Stress Disorder.

Obsessive-Compulsive Disorder (OCD)

OCD is characterized by a pattern of unwanted thoughts and worries (obsessions) that may cause the OCD sufferer to engage in repeated behaviors (compulsions). These compulsive thoughts and behaviors can disrupt everyday life and cause severe anguish. Those who suffer from OCD might try to suppress or disregard their obsessions and compulsions, but doing so tends to make them feel more anxious and upset. Because of this, many OCD sufferers become compelled to engage in obsessive behaviors in an effort to reduce their tension and anxiety. Despite attempts to disregard bothersome impulses or desires, these impulses often linger until the OCD sufferer performs the ritualistic compulsion. As you can see, it's a vicious cycle.

Adjustment Disorder

Adjustment Disorder is a temporary and common condition. It's also known as situational depression. An individual who displays an exaggerated response to a stressful or upsetting event will oftentimes be diagnosed with Adjustment Disorder. Adjustment Disorder can be caused by one singular incident (such as a painful divorce) or several separate events (such as work problems, financial issues, and health scares). These stressors can affect a single person, a household, or an entire community (think natural disasters, for example).

Selective Mutism

Do you know someone who's able to talk freely and frequently at home, but freezes up when faced with social situations in public settings? A person with Selective Mutism experiences extreme anxiety in certain social situations and is unable to communicate in particular social settings (i.e. at work). In other contexts, like at home with family, people with Selective Mutism are usually able to talk comfortably and communicate well with those around them.

MISCONCEPTIONS ABOUT ANXIETY

While anxiety is extremely common, it's also quite misunderstood. Plenty of misinformation has been spread about anxiety and anxiety disorders, which has made the stigma surrounding anxiety that much more harmful to those who experience it. You've probably already heard some of the misconceptions about anxiety I've listed below, but if you haven't, this is generally what the misinformed believe:

Anxiety Isn't an Actual Illness

Yeah, and Covid-19 isn't an actual illness either! Just kidding. It totally is, and so is anxiety. Many people don't realize that anxiety disorders go far beyond the general worries people experience in their everyday lives. The Diagnostic and Statistical Manual for Mental Health, Fifth Edition (DSM-5) requires a specific set of symptoms to be present for at least six months in order for someone to be diagnosed with an anxiety disorder. A person suffering from an anxiety disorder may experience severe disability and distress in their everyday life.

Anxiety is Just a Phase

If anyone's ever told you this, they're gaslighting you (unintentionally or otherwise). Certain circumstances or stages of life may cause a person's worry levels to rise or fall. A person with an anxiety disorder, however, might occasionally experience a small improvement in symptoms or be able to get back to some of their usual activities. This might give some the impression that their anxiety disorder is no longer present or that the symptoms are "gone." However, anxiety disorders can be persistent and long-lasting, and if they're not treated properly, symptoms will probably return.

Panic Attacks Always Result in Fainting

No two people will experience a panic attack in exactly the same way. A panic attack can cause a variety of symptoms, including breathing problems and a racing pulse. Although these symptoms are uncommon during panic attacks, some people may pass out or puke, which can heighten the anxiety they're already experiencing. The fear of passing out can occasionally make panicky feelings worse. The act of actually fainting during a panic attack, however, is a very severe reaction, and it rarely happens.

People With Anxiety Should Just Avoid Things That Make Them Anxious

This is known as avoidance, which is actually a common symptom of anxiety. Needless to say, stressful situations can be particularly unpleasant for someone who's suffering from an anxiety disorder. Life is full of stressful situations, and developing effective coping mechanisms to help yourself cope with your anxious feelings in these situations is an essential part of managing your anxiety. In other words, you shouldn't avoid the things that make you anxious... you should confront them head-on!

It's Obvious When Someone Has an Anxiety Disorder

Contrary to popular belief, a lot of people are really, *really* good at hiding their anxiety. Most of the time, another person's anxiety will be completely invisible to you. This is especially true of people who suffer from high-functioning anxiety. On the other hand, some people might struggle to conceal their symptoms because they feel worried about others noticing or calling attention to them. It really just depends on the person.

Breathing into a Paper Bag Prevents Hyperventilation

You've undoubtedly seen this on T.V. or in a movie. A person who's hyperventilating breathes into a paper bag and it helps to calm them down. Although breathing into a paper bag can serve as a visual aid for people who are hyperventilating, it can also limit your oxygen supply. This could end up making your anxiety worse, as you'll be even shorter of breath. You'll be much better suited doing some mindful breathing exercises in the open air.

Medication Is the Only Way to Manage Anxiety

Anxiety disorders come in many different forms, which means treatment options can vary significantly. Typically, a combination of medication and Cognitive Behavior Therapy (CBT) is helpful for most people. However, taking medication is not the only way to treat anxiety. The most effective course of treatment for any given patient will rely on the nature and intensity of their anxiety disorder, as well as their unique circumstances and preferences.

ANXIETY LOOK-ALIKES

Again, anxiety has many faces. It also has many clones! Listed below are some health problems that professionals may misdiagnose as anxiety:

- Heart problems
- Endocrine issues
- Asthma
- Diabetes
- Hyperthyroidism
- Sleep apnea
- Adrenal dysfunction/ Adrenal insufficiency
- Irritable bowel syndrome (IBS)
- Electrolyte imbalance
- Neurological conditions
- Postural Orthostatic Tachycardia Syndrome (POTS)
- Inappropriate Sinus Tachycardia (IST)
- Lung diseases
- Fibromyalgia
- Endometriosis
- Lyme Disease
- Ankylosing Spondylitis (AS)

- Crohn's Disease
- Polycystic Ovarian Syndrome (PCOS)

If you feel like you've been misdiagnosed, it can't hurt to get a second opinion from a different doctor. Trust your gut and look out for yourself!

SEGUE

As you can see, anxiety disorders come in a variety of shapes and sizes. Anxiety is the beast with many faces, and it can oftentimes be difficult to diagnose. The misconceptions surrounding anxiety don't make things any easier for anxiety sufferers either. However, it's important to remember that anxiety is treatable and all hope is not lost. In the next chapter, I'll dive deeper into anxiety and give you a chance to reflect on your past and current experiences with it. Remember: anxiety is a journey and this journey affects different people in different ways.

2

THE "I" IN THE MIDDLE OF ANXIETY

> 66 *"How much pain has cost us the evils which have never happened."*
>
> — THOMAS JEFFERSON

C an you remember the first time you experienced feeling anxious? Maybe you felt nervous and excited at the same time when you woke up on Christmas morning as a kid, or perhaps you used to get a stomachache before your sports competitions in high school. The latter describes my earliest and most memorable experience with severe anxiety. I ran cross country throughout high school and college, and I would always, *always* get sick right before a big race.

As I discussed in the previous chapter, anxiety takes many different forms. It doesn't always look how you expect it to look, and it doesn't always feel how you expect it to feel. Most of the time, telling yourself "I'm just nervous," or "it's just anxiety" doesn't make your anxiety go away (at least, in my experience). People with anxiety disorders, who literally *cannot* calm down just by taking logic and reason into account, might wonder what the heck is going on if they've never been properly diagnosed.

Whenever my friend, Charles, was dealing with a particularly brutal bout of anxiety, he would freeze up. When his girlfriend asked him what was wrong, he'd say: "I just need to stay perfectly still right now," and, like a statue in an earthquake, he would stand ramrod straight and tremble uncontrollably. Charles's girlfriend became concerned and started looking into some grounding exercises. *"Can you tell me five things you can see?"* She'd ask him. *"Can you tell me five things you can hear?"* This helped a little, but it was a bandaid, not a cure.

Charles needed to reflect on his journey and his experiences with anxiety if he was going to confront it head-on. Although he appreciated his friends and his girlfriend being there for him, he was ultimately the one who had to help himself — and he did! It may have taken him a lot of time and effort to overcome his anxiety, but based on how well he's doing today, he would definitely agree it was worth it.

One of the main things that helped Charles reflect on his anxiety journey was writing about it. He started carrying a small journal around with him everywhere, and when he had a spare moment, he would sit down and record his thoughts. If he had something on his mind — a past experience that made him anxious, or an upcoming future stressor — he would take the time to ask himself certain questions (i.e. "What was making me feel anxious in that particular situation?" "What is making me feel this way now?"). Doing this allowed Charles to take control of his own thoughts and confront his anxiety. It helped him better understand himself, which in turn helped him gain a deeper understanding of his anxious thoughts and feelings.

While engaging with this chapter, I'd like to invite you to dig deep. Consider your personal journey with anxiety. How old were you when you first started experiencing a lot of anxiety? What are some of the things that make you feel most anxious now that you're an adult? Identifying your triggers and putting in the work to understand them is an important step in the process of overcoming your anxiety. It certainly won't be a walk in the park, but it *will* be worth it.

COMMON SYMPTOMS OF ANXIETY

We've already gone over some common anxiety symptoms, but it can't hurt to reiterate. The more you understand about your anxiety, the more success you'll have while confronting it. For this reason, I'd like to delve into some lesser-known symptoms of anxiety as well. Plenty of people are familiar with symptoms like sweaty palms and a churning stomach, but most aren't aware of some of the rarer anxiety symptoms — such as excessive yawning, pins and needles, and depersonalization. Let's get into it, shall we?

Physical Effects

When you're dealing with severe anxiety, it can sometimes feel like you're experiencing a major health issue. As I discussed previously, this is why anxiety sometimes gets misdiagnosed. The common physical effects of anxiety include nausea, dizziness, an increased heart rate, dry mouth, rapid breathing (also known as hyperventilation), shortness of breath, sweating (especially cold sweats), tingling hands and feet, trembling, tense muscles, pins and needles, feeling weak, insomnia, grinding your teeth, and gastrointestinal (GI) issues.

It can be quite a lot to deal with! Although, it's important to note that most people with anxiety won't experience all of these symptoms at the same time. For example, you're more likely to grind your teeth at night while you're sleeping, and you might not experience rarer symptoms like pins and needles or tingling hands and feet at all. Some people with anxiety might burst into tears or groan as if they're in pain. Some panic attacks may require a trip to the emergency room or another type of medical intervention.

Psychological Effect

When it comes to the psychological effects of anxiety, things get a bit more complicated. Most psychological effects are invisible to others, and are oftentimes misunderstood by health professionals who aren't well-versed in mental health. People with anxiety who are experiencing psychological symptoms will typically have a difficult time articulating these types of symptoms, especially in the midst of a panic attack. Some common psychological symptoms of anxiety include trouble concentrating, avoiding things that trigger anxiety, an inability to relax, having a sense of dread or feeling like something terrible will happen, feeling like the world is speeding up or slowing down, and worrying about anxiety itself.

People experiencing the psychological effects of anxiety will often seek reassurance from other people, or worry that they're losing touch with reality. Most will fall into a depressed mood and ruminate on the bad things that have happened to them. Another, less common psychological symptom is depersonalization, which essentially means feeling disconnected from your mind and body. Derealization is a relatively rare symptom as well. It's described as the feeling of being disconnected from the world around you, which can be quite scary.

Other Uncommon Symptoms of Anxiety

Many people associate the word "anxiety" with uneasiness, an inability to sit still, sweating, or an increased heart rate. While these symptoms are common, they are not the only indications that someone is experiencing anxiety. Some people may experience anxiety in unusual ways and may never end up experiencing the more prevalent symptoms of anxiety. Some of the more uncommon symptoms of anxiety include chest pain, fatigue, brain shivers or "zaps," hives or skin rashes, tinnitus (a phantom ringing in the ears), excessive yawning, jaw pain, perfectionism, indecisiveness, cold hands and feet, and circulation problems.

If you find yourself experiencing one of these symptoms, you may want to have a professional evaluate you for an anxiety disorder. These symptoms are problematic anyway, healthwise, so it might be a good idea to see a doctor anyway. Something you definitely *shouldn't* do is look up your symptoms on the internet. People with anxiety oftentimes feel compelled to do this out of desperation for an immediate answer, but there's a lot of misinformation out there. Googling your symptoms is likely to make you feel more anxious, so it's best to avoid doing that at all costs.

HOW YOUR ANXIETY COULD BE AFFECTING YOU

As I've already discussed, anxiety is a perfectly normal response to stress. This response starts in the Amygdala, which is the area of your brain that transmits distress signals to the hypothalamus. Your body receives these signals, which triggers a "fight, flight, or freeze" response. Everyone responds to stressful situations differently (which, of course, is psychologically fascinating). The "fight, flight, or freeze" response is generally a good thing, but it can end up causing issues if your body "freezes" in a situation where you should have fought back.

If you suffer from an anxiety disorder, it's going to affect you differently than run-of-the-mill anxiety does. Long-term stress responses to anxiety can end up causing negative emotional and physical reactions in your body. In other words, anxiety takes more of a mental and physical toll than you might think. Let's take a closer look at how anxiety can impact and alter your various bodily and brain systems below:

Central Nervous System

Your brain is a delicate and complicated organ. If you suffer from chronic anxiety, your brain is going to be releasing stress hormones far more often than it should. You may experience headaches, vertigo, and depressive symptoms more frequently as a result. Basically, when you're feeling anxious, your brain fills your central nervous system with hormones and chemicals meant to help you react to a specific danger. Long-term exposure to these hormones (mainly adrenaline and cortisol) can be detrimental to your physical and mental health.

Cardiovascular System

Those with anxiety disorders oftentimes suffer from heart palpitations, an increased heart rate, and chest pain. When these symptoms occur, your body is under an immense amount of stress. It's essentially working really hard to pump adrenaline and cortisol into your system so that you can effectively deal with whatever your brain is perceiving as threatening. This may increase your risk of experiencing a heart attack, especially if you already have heart problems.

Gastrointestinal System

Stomachaches, nausea, and vomiting are some of the most common symptoms anxiety patients experience. A lot of people will also experience a loss of appetite. Studies show that anxiety and irritable bowel syndrome (IBS) could be connected, which makes sense because anxiety negatively impacts your gastrointestinal system. If you're constantly having diarrhea or throwing up, your GI system will never have a chance to fully heal. So, if anxiety is what's causing you to have these symptoms, it's very important that you address it.

Immune System

When your body is under too much stress, it can negatively affect your immune system. It's crucial that your immune system remains in good shape because it's what helps you fight off diseases and viruses that can make you very sick. A person with chronic stress and anxiety, however, will typically have a weakened immune system because their body never truly returns to its normal functioning. This unfortunately puts anxiety sufferers at risk of developing infections and illnesses more frequently.

Respiratory System

Hyperventilation is common in some people who experience panic attacks. This can put a lot of stress on a person's respiratory system, and if you have a condition like Chronic Obstructive Pulmonary Disease (COPD), the rapid breathing that comes with anxiety can make your symptoms much worse. This can sometimes result in hospitalization or a trip to the emergency room.

TIPS TO HELP YOU IDENTIFY YOUR TRIGGERS

Most of the time, your anxiety is being triggered by something — whether you're aware of it or not. It can be difficult to identify your specific triggers, especially considering the fact that there could be a lot going on (in your surroundings and in your head) whilst you're experiencing anxious feelings or a panic attack. This, in and of itself, could be an anxiety trigger for you. When it comes to overcoming anxiety, identifying and understanding your triggers is an incredibly important step. If you're not sure where to start, don't worry. That's why I'm here!

Learn the Original Root of Your Anxiety

Pinpointing the original root of your anxiety can be tricky. It might be beneficial for you to seek guidance from a therapist, as they should be able to help you access memories that are buried deep within you. Before you start digging for the root of your anxiety, though, you're going to want to manage your anxiety symptoms. If you're currently feeling anxious, try placing one hand on your chest and the other on your belly. As you breathe in and out, pay attention to when each of your hands goes up and down. You can do this standing up, sitting down, or lying on your bed.

From there, I suggest sitting in a comfortable position with your journal in front of you. Start writing about your past experiences with anxiety, and identify the moment or moments that you believe are continuing to contribute to your anxiety today. Try to dig deep. Consider your childhood and your teenagehood. A lot happens while you're growing up, and it's surprisingly easy to suppress negative memories as an adult. As you're writing, try to identify what you're truly afraid of as well as why you're afraid of it. This should help you figure a few things out!

Think Back to What Triggered You in the Past

Although this process might be unpleasant, it's completely necessary. Remember, you can always have a therapist walk you through this process if it makes you feel uncomfortable to do it on your own. Identifying your past triggers is also a crucial part of PTSD treatment, and hey, your anxiety could very well be intensifying possible PTSD symptoms (or vice versa). That said, it's important to remember that PTSD isn't always a result of a big traumatic event. Some people experience PTSD symptoms as a result of the build-up of small traumas that have shattered certain beliefs they once held dear.

Look into Your Home Life

Childhood is a particularly delicate stage of life. You're forming your sense of self and developing what will later become your core beliefs during this time. Although exploring your childhood and past home life can be emotionally draining, it's incredibly important. Keep in mind that looking back and reflecting on your home life isn't about blaming your parents, yourself, or the town you grew up in. It's about acknowledging the fact that your loved ones probably did their best with what they had, all things considered. In your journal, respond to the following questions in regard to your childhood and home life:

- What were my relationships like with my family members?
- Were there times that I felt ignored, shamed, punished, ridiculed, or afraid?
- Did I ever feel like I wasn't good enough?
- Did I ever feel like it wasn't okay to express myself?

Consider Your Habits

Did you know that certain bad habits can trigger anxiety in some people? This is more common than you might think. Habits like drinking, smoking, and avoiding conflict can actually make your anxiety worse. It can be difficult for some to identify which habits could be contributing to their anxiety, but reflecting can work wonders. In your journal, reflect on the following questions. As you're writing, remember to take note of when your anxiety usually happens, where it happens, and how long your symptoms last:

- Has my anxiety (of the intensity of my anxiety) increased recently?
- Have my habits changed recently?

- How are my sleep habits?
- Have I been drinking or smoking more? How do I usually feel after drinking or smoking?

List Your Fears

This can be a great way to pinpoint some of the things that are continuously triggering your anxious feelings. Try not to think too hard about it. Just write down the first things that come to mind. While writing, try not to judge yourself based on your fears. Everyone is afraid of something, and facing your fears is totally possible (especially if you identify them first).

Pinpoint Patterns

Confronting your anxiety is like playing an elaborate game of connect-the-dots. In order to effectively overcome your anxiety, you're going to need to obtain a sense of understanding about yourself (i.e. how and why you operate the way you do). Pinpointing your anxiety patterns can be an excellent way to identify and understand the ways in which anxiety has impacted your life. In your journal, respond to the following questions:

- How long has it been since I felt differently (i.e. less anxious) than I do now?
- What has changed in my life over the past 3-6 months? How much has changed in a year?
- Were there other times in my life when I've felt anxious, but the situation was different?
- If yes, what happened? Is there a common thread between these situations?

Consider Therapy

There's a lot of social stigma surrounding therapy, but in reality, there's absolutely nothing wrong with going to see a therapist when you need help managing your emotions. A therapist is a trained professional, and their job is not to judge you. Everyone could benefit from talking to a therapist sometimes, but weekly or bi-weekly therapy might be ideal if you're really struggling.

Be Honest With Yourself (But Be Kind to Yourself)

Facing your fears and anxiety triggers is no easy task. Trust me, I get it. Although it might be hard, being honest with yourself and the people you confide in (i.e. your therapist, your friends, your family, etc) is one of the best things you can do to help yourself overcome your anxiety issues. If you can't be honest with yourself, you won't be able to get to the root of what's been causing your problems in the first place.

You should also, of course, be kind to yourself. Identifying your triggers can cause quite a bit of mental strain, so it's important to take breaks every now and then. Don't be too hard on yourself, either. It's fairly common for people with anxiety to ruminate on their past errors and experiences, but this is ultimately not productive. Practice self-compassion and be mindful of those around you. Take a deep breath, and surround yourself with love. You deserve it!

SEGUE

The symptoms of anxiety are plentiful, and some symptoms in particular can be rather difficult to deal with. Identifying and understanding your symptoms can be quite helpful, as can identifying and understanding your triggers. In the next chapter, I'll go over some of the main anxiety triggers adults experience, as well as what you can do to combat these triggers.

3

TRIGGER 1: WHEN LIFE THROWS YOU CURVEBALLS...

> *"Life is 10% of what you experience and 90% of how you respond to it."*

— DOROTHY M. NEDDERMEYER

When you start to feel anxious, it's usually because you're being triggered by something. You may not be aware of it at first, but the trigger is there, lurking beneath the things that tend to pile up in the forefront of your mind: money, family, your physical health, and work. Chances are, you've become so accustomed to carrying these weights on your shoulders that you've stopped noticing how heavy they are. Even if everything is going relatively well with work, your family life, your health, and your financials, it's a lot to balance — and this balancing act itself can be stressful.

If you're suffering from an anxiety disorder, it can feel like the end of the world when one single thing goes wrong. My friend, Charles, could tell you this firsthand. When he was in his mid-twenties, everything was going swimmingly with his job, his relationship, and his physical health. He had gotten a promotion recently, and was thinking about proposing to his then-girlfriend. Obviously, he was over the moon that things were going so well for him, but an anxious thought lingered at the back of his mind at all times: "Okay, so when is the bad thing going to happen? When is all of this going to fall apart?"

People with anxiety tend to have a heightened sense of how fragile human life is. There's this constant fear that everything is going to come crashing down all at once. Perhaps you've felt this fear before. I know I have. When a person with anxiety gets triggered by a stressful life event, or even something small — like turning in an assignment a few hours late at work — their anxiety will often snowball. It will get very big very fast, which usually makes the anxiety-sufferer feel even more overwhelmed.

Charles, like many people with anxiety, developed an unhealthy coping mechanism, which likely coincided with or caused his depressed feelings. Instead of enjoying all of the good things in his life, he obsessed about when everything was going to turn sour. He anticipated things turning sour because in his eyes "they always did." He felt that his obsessive anticipation gave him relief from his anxiety because "if you anticipate that bad things will happen to you, you won't be surprised when they do."

It took him a long time to figure out that this was not a very good way to live. This coping mechanism gave him the illusion of control, but in reality, his anxiety still had control over him. Despite the fact that most things in his life were going well, Charles was miserable. "It was almost like I didn't know how to enjoy things," he would tell me later, once he started to figure himself out. "My brain wouldn't let me."

What eventually helped Charles help himself was this: he identified his triggers, and learned how to manage them effectively. In this chapter, I'll be going over a few of the main stressors that tend to trigger people with anxiety disorders. This should help you gain a deeper understanding of how these various life challenges are affecting you — as well as what you can do to help yourself when you're feeling anxious in the midst of life's many curveballs.

MONEY PROBLEMS

In this day and age, a lot of people feel like they're working more than ever, yet somehow they're still losing money. This is the result of late-stage capitalism mixed with poor financial literacy. Young people, in particular, were never taught how to properly manage their finances, which means the majority of them have developed some rather unhealthy spending habits. Inflation is a very real thing as well, and it's something that's been causing almost everyone immense stress — especially considering the current cost of living.

What It Can Feel Like

A number of factors can trigger financial anxiety. Oftentimes, it's not just about lacking money. People with financial anxiety frequently worry about their bills. They may be reluctant to check their bank accounts or deal with anything related to money at all, for that matter. Although financial anxiety might seem normal (everyone worries about money once in a while), it's just as serious as other types of anxiety. Financial anxiety can cause physical health problems, such as difficulty sleeping, trouble concentrating, and a loss of appetite. It's definitely not something you want to ignore.

What It Can Look Like

Overspending

You'd think that being concerned about money would make you more inclined to save it, but shopping can actually give you relief from your anxiety, so many people use it as a coping mechanism. The problem is, spending more money in an attempt to find relief will just make your money situation worse.

Hoarding

Excessive spending can oftentimes result in hoarding. People tend to seek solace in material possessions, and because of this, some will end up buying a lot of useless things without ever throwing anything away. This hoarding behavior is usually somewhat obsessive, and although it can be calming in the short term, it's not particularly healthy.

Fear of Spending

Being overly thrifty is essentially the opposite of hoarding. Saving your money in an exceptionally obsessive way could prevent you from taking vacations or providing yourself with a comfortable living situation. Some people who are afraid of spending might skip out on things like medical treatment and necessary car maintenance. This form of anxiety can also affect those who overwork or work compulsively in order to increase their income.

Uncontrollable Finances

Those who experience financial anxiety might be uncomfortable making and saving money. This can have a devastating effect on things like retirement planning, or saving up for a future home. This form of financial anxiety can make it impossible for anxiety sufferers to budget properly, which, of course, only serves to make their financial anxiety worse.

Depression

A person with financial anxiety will often experience depressed feelings about the world around them. They might feel like nothing ever goes right for them, money-wise, and that budgeting and saving are impossible due to things like inflation and capitalism. While inflation and capitalism do make things difficult for most people, these things do not make budgeting and saving *impossible*. Those with financial anxiety will have a hard time realizing this, however.

What Can You Do?

If you're struggling with financial anxiety, just know that you're not alone. Plenty of people all over the world are currently dealing with this form of anxiety, and the triggers — prices going up, budget cuts, expensive health scares, downsizing, etc — can be crushing and constant. Thankfully, there are a number of things you can do if you've been feeling anxious about your finances. Let's go over some financial strategies that should help to alleviate some of the anxiety you've been experiencing below.

Set Financial Goals

If you're dealing with financial anxiety, one of the best things you can do for yourself is set some solid financial goals. Decide that you're going to save a certain amount of money by a specific date, and start setting it aside in a savings account or piggy bank. Even if you're only able to set aside $10 per month, that's still better than nothing. It's amazing how anxiety-relieving having some savings can be!

Keep Track of Your Spending

It can be difficult to keep track of your spending, especially with things like automatic payments for monthly subscriptions being a major factor. People with financial anxiety might not *want* to keep track of their spending because paying attention to that sort of thing can be anxiety-inducing. However, you're going to be much better off in the long run if you keep track of your spending habits and avoid spending too much money on things you don't really need. That way, you'll be able to save and eventually relieve your financial anxiety.

Make a Financial Plan... and Stick to It

If you've been struggling with finances, the first thing you're going to want to do is identify your various financial problems and pain points. Are you attempting to live outside of your means? Do you have any monthly subscriptions — such as Netflix and Hulu — that you'd feel comfortable living without? Once you identify the source of what's been draining your money, you'll be able to come up with a financial plan and put that plan into action. Remember to monitor your progress, and don't get discouraged by setbacks. It's a marathon, not a sprint.

Create a Budget

What are your monthly spending habits like? Do you always set aside money for things like rent and bills, or do you spend as you see fit and hope for the best? If it's the latter, don't worry. I've been there too, and I know how hard it can be to change your bad spending habits. The easiest way to do so is to create a weekly or monthly budget. Sit down and figure out how much money you're going to spend on your necessities (i.e. rent, food, bills, doctor's appointments, etc.) Then, you can determine how much of your budget you're going to contribute to your savings account, your emergency fund — and finally — things like takeout, clothes, and video games.

Manage Your Debt

It's difficult for most people to live a full life without accumulating some debt here and there. If you happen to have student debt or credit card debt looming over you, just know that there are ways to effectively manage this. It's important that you contribute a small part of your weekly or monthly budget to paying off your debts, as you don't want them to keep accumulating interest. If need be, you can create an extra source of income for yourself — such as dog walking or renting out an extra room in your house. This will help you save up enough money to eventually pay off your debts.

Create an Emergency Fund

There's nothing more stressful than not having enough money to pay for healthcare, house maintenance, or car maintenance when an emergency occurs. Emergencies can be scary, and they usually come out of nowhere. You never know when you're going to have to rush your significant other to the emergency room or take your pet to the vet for emergency surgery. These things happen, but setting up an emergency fund will ensure that you'll be able to take care of the financial side of things when they do.

Don't Compare Yourself to Others

It's perfectly natural to compare yourself to others, especially with the prevalence of social media and wealthy influencers showing off their luxurious lifestyles. It's very important, however, that you don't compare your life to the lives of people on social media. Most of the time, social media is a facade. People aren't going to share the *bad* parts of their lives on Instagram. They're only going to share the highlights. Chances are, they're struggling just as much as you are (even if that struggle isn't financial in nature).

GRIEF

When you're grieving, it can oftentimes feel like you've lost all sense of control — which, of course, can feed your anxiety. The passing of a loved one is always stressful and sad. It's perfectly normal (and healthy) to grieve, but if you've been through insurmountable grief in your life, it has probably taken a toll on both your physical and mental health. Those who have lost someone dear to them will typically be reluctant to get close to someone else in the same way after the fact. Those with terminally ill parents or siblings may have a heightened sense of anxiety due to anticipatory grief. The fear of losing a particular loved one may loom over them and cause them to feel on edge.

Grief is a huge, complicated emotion, and it's not something the average person can healthily deal with if they don't have a good support system. When I lost my best friend to cancer, I didn't know how to cope. The fact that the world kept moving forward after she was gone seemed absurd to me. It made me angry for a long time, and then, for even longer, it made me sad. She passed away almost a decade ago, and it *still* makes me sad. I've come to realize, though, that she would want me to accept her death and move on with my life. Of course, this is easier said than done. I'm probably always going to have a hole in my heart, but I'm learning how to patch it up. Slowly but surely.

I'm not telling you this story to make you sad, or to trigger you in any way. I just want you to know that you're not alone. One thing I've noticed about the topic of grief is that we don't talk about it enough. Talking about grief might be painful — especially for those who have lost someone — but it's an incredibly important part of the healing process. So, let's talk about it.

What It Can Feel Like

Grief is a natural reaction to loss. It tends to go hand in hand with anxiety, especially in the early stages (i.e. denial, anger, and bargaining). From there, one will typically slip into depression, which is the longest stage of grief for most people. The final stage of grief, as you may or may not know, is acceptance. It's important to keep in mind, however, that just because you've accepted the death of the person or pet you've been grieving, that doesn't mean you're done grieving forever. Anyone who's lost someone knows it's more complicated than that.

Those who are grieving might feel unsafe or like they don't have control in certain situations. They might start to feel anxious about their own health, or the health of their loved ones. Some people who are going through the cycle of grief might lash out at others, or avoid social situations. It's important to note that everyone experiences grief differently. You might feel numb after a loved one passes, or you might feel overwhelmed with emotion. That — in part — is what makes grief such a significant anxiety trigger.

What It Can Look Like

Denial

For a person who's just lost someone, it can be difficult to face reality. Losing someone you love can be an extreme shock to the system, and it's only natural to feel like everything is slipping through your fingers all of a sudden. Those who have recently lost someone might stay in a state of denial for quite some time. It's a common coping mechanism, but it is oftentimes short-lived.

Anger

The next stage in the grief cycle is usually anger. After losing someone you love, it's normal to feel angry about the lack of control you have over the situation. You might feel like life isn't fair, and that the whole world is trash without that person in it. I know that's how I felt when I lost my friend. In this stage, you may lash out at others and burst into tears at random times. This stage can be difficult, but remember to breathe. This too shall pass.

Bargaining

In order to feel more in control of the situation, or to more effectively cope with your loss, you might attempt to bargain with the truth. This stage is similar to denial, although it's a bit more complicated. You may get nervous, irritable, and eventually depressed when you realize that some of the "what ifs" you've been entertaining wouldn't have prevented the loss from happening.

Depression

The depression stage is probably what most people think of when they think of grief. This stage tends to be quite long, and for a lot of people, it's the most difficult stage of grief to get through. When in the depression stage, you might experience bouts of intense sadness and isolate yourself from others. You may feel fearful about what's going to happen next, which, in turn, can amplify your anxiety.

Acceptance

Once you learn how to accept the reality of your loss, you'll be able to focus on healing. Acceptance is a leap of faith. It's a huge mountain to climb over, and a lot of people can't do it alone. The steps that follow the grieving process might make some people feel anxious because they know that they're going to be entering into a period of significant change. Some may feel like everything is changing too fast, and that they're not ready to let go quite yet. This is understandably anxiety-inducing, but coping mechanisms like attending talk therapy and practicing self-care can help.

What Can You Do?

Remember, the grieving process is normal and healthy — just so long as you have the tools to effectively manage your emotions once you've been through all of the stages of the grief cycle. It's possible for some people with anxiety to be diagnosed with prolonged grief disorder, which is essentially a complicated form of grief that takes an abnormally long time to go away. This is relatively rare, and most of the time, it's a trauma response. However, it's still something to be aware of. Let's go over some strategies you can try out if you've been having a difficult time coping with your grief below.

Make Space for Grief

The last thing you want to do is bottle up painful emotions. Although shoving your emotions under the rug may feel easier at first, it's ultimately going to make your anxiety and depression worse. Grief is your body's way of handling the unique stress that comes with losing a loved one, and it's healthy for you to experience the emotions that accompany it. I've mentioned, a few times now, the importance of confronting your anxiety head-on. Confronting your feelings of grief head-on is a big part of confronting your anxiety as a whole.

Practice Self-Care

When you're going through a grieving period, it can be difficult to take proper care of yourself. This is especially true during the depression stage. You might lose your appetite or feel unable to practice good personal hygiene during this time. Although it might be hard, practicing self-care can make you feel a whole lot better. Even just taking a shower and putting on some clean clothes can work wonders. Getting yourself outside and breathing in the fresh air might help as well.

Write About Your Grief

If you're not sure how to process your grief, try writing about it. Writing can be a great way to organize your thoughts and emotions, and it's a fantastic form of self-expression, too. You might find it therapeutic to keep a journal and track your emotions throughout your grieving process. If you enjoy creative writing, you might gain some solace from writing a poem or a creative essay about the person you've lost. This would also be a wonderful way to pay homage to that person.

Seek Out Support and Connection

Grief counseling can be exceptionally helpful. Sometimes, what a person going through the grief cycle needs most is someone to talk to. A good grief counselor will be able to help you manage your complicated emotions as well as provide you with effective coping tools. It's also a good idea to stay connected with your other loved ones. For example, if you and your friend both knew the person who passed away, your friend might be going through their own grieving process. Grieving together can be therapeutic in comparison to grieving alone, so don't be afraid to reach out to them.

SEVERE ILLNESS DIAGNOSIS/HEALTH PROBLEMS

Whether it's a chronic or life-threatening condition, like cancer, or a significant health event — like a stroke, heart attack, or immobilizing injury — getting diagnosed with a serious health problem can be incredibly disruptive and anxiety-inducing. Most major health problems seem to appear out of nowhere, and they can completely derail your life.

If you've been diagnosed with a serious health problem, you may feel paralyzed by shock or overwhelmed with the sense that you'll never be able to properly cope with your illness. Some might feel numb or emotionally exhausted, and some might respond with denial, anger, or bargaining (i.e. some might experience the five stages of grief). The inner turmoil you feel after getting a serious diagnosis might make it difficult for you to think clearly or perform your daily tasks at work. In some cases, being diagnosed with a chronic health problem can cause a person to develop depression or an anxiety disorder.

What It Can Feel Like

Life changes are scary for a lot of people, and being diagnosed with a serious illness is one of the biggest life changes a person can go through. Those who are in this situation might worry about the future. They might grieve the loss of their old life, and be unable to look past the worst-case scenario. Some may worry about what will happen to their loved ones after they're gone, and some may become obsessed with death and the dying process. All of this, of course, can mess with your brain in a big way — so much so that it can contribute to the deterioration of your physical health.

What It Can Look Like

People who have been diagnosed with a serious health problem may try to avoid thinking about death and dying at all costs. They might get dizzy, or experience panic attacks when they think about dying because the possibility of death has suddenly become all too real. Some people might become obsessive about requesting medical tests and going to doctor's appointments more often than they need to. They might become depressed, or feel frustrated with their situation — which is understandable. However, living out the rest of your days in a state of despair is not ideal, which is why I've listed some effective coping strategies below.

What Can You Do?

Understand Your Condition

Gaining a deeper understanding of your condition may alleviate some of the fear and stress you're feeling about it. The more you understand something, the less scary it will seem. It's important that you ask your doctor questions and be patient with the pace of your treatment and recovery. Seek support from others when you need it, and be open to the changes that are about to happen in your life. Take a deep breath. The situation is not ideal, but you're going to have an easier time dealing with it if you learn to accept it.

Explore Your Emotions

Participating in activities like making mind maps and journaling daily can help you explore and more effectively manage your emotions. Doing this can help you distinguish between your worries that are solvable and your worries that are unsolvable. Writing in a journal is also a great way to process your emotions. You'll have an easier time keeping track of your thoughts, which should help you figure out what you're really thinking and feeling about all of this.

Pursue Activities That Bring You Joy

When you're dealing with a serious illness, it can be helpful to distract yourself. This might be a good time to pick up a hobby you've been neglecting for a long time — such as painting or bird watching. You may be inclined to learn something new, or you may gain a newfound appreciation for nature. Enjoy the little things, and spend time with the people you love most. Talk to others about your thoughts and emotions, and spread joy wherever you can. Take care of yourself and be responsible for your own happiness. Trust me. It'll help.

LOSING A JOB

Losing your job can be extremely stressful. Your job is likely how you support yourself and your family. You know that without it you might not be able to do things like pay rent or put dinner on the table. Looking for a job can be equally as stressful, especially if you're scrambling to find work after getting downsized or replaced by an automated system. If you've lost your job recently, you might feel downtrodden and anxious about the future. You might be questioning your identity, which is a symptom that tends to accompany feeling powerless. Let's talk more about the unique stress that comes with losing a job below.

What It Can Feel Like

Losing a job often comes with its own grieving process. You may miss the structure that work gave you, or feel a loss of control over the direction your life is headed. Some people going through unemployment will find themselves feeling hopeless and insecure after losing a job. They might feel betrayed by their employer, or they might blame *themselves* for losing their job in the first place — which is actually rather in line with the symptoms of anxiety and depression. You may feel even worse if the job loss *was* somehow your fault, but listen: everyone makes mistakes, and a lot of employers do not (for whatever reason) allow room for human error. Don't ruminate on it. That will only make things worse.

What It Can Look Like

Those who are going through unemployment may experience physical symptoms due to the stress and anxiety they might be feeling. These symptoms may include depression, insomnia, back pain, headaches, and high blood pressure. Some might get into the habit of self-medicating with drugs or alcohol, and some might spend most of their days "sick in bed." Remember, losing a job comes with its own grieving process. It's perfectly natural to lose the will to take proper care of yourself for a little while, but this is a dangerous road to go down. Let's talk about what you can do if you've recently lost a job and are having a difficult time coping with the anxiety that comes with that.

What Can You Do?

Face Your Feelings

If you've lost a job recently, you're probably experiencing a lot of complicated feelings. It's very important that you allow yourself to *feel* these feelings rather than bottle them up. Try not to beat yourself up about the job loss, and look for any silver linings in the situation. Perhaps you were unhappy in that position, anyway, and now you have the opportunity to find a better job. If you'd like to, you can write about your feelings in your journal. This will help you accept reality and avoid internalizing your feelings of rejection.

Seek Out a Support System

You shouldn't have to go through the stress of unemployment alone. Try to think of this as an opportunity to reconnect with old friends or open up to your family members. If you're feeling ready to find new employment, join a job club and network to create meaningful connections. Spend time with those you love most, and try to let go of the things you can't control. There's no sense in spending all of your time worrying about the future of your employment because that's not something you can control during all hours of the day. Take the time to relax with your friends and family. You deserve to do so.

Find Other Ways to Define Yourself

This might be a good time to pick up a new hobby or get back into something you enjoyed previously but haven't really had time to engage in because of work.

Go on camping trips with your friends, and start writing that novel you've been putting off. Volunteer at your local humane society, and get into a new routine to keep yourself busy. As cheesy as it may sound, life is for the living. Just because you're unemployed, that doesn't mean you have to put your life on hold. Get out there, and live it to the fullest.

Practice Radical Acceptance

Radical acceptance is all about accepting the fact that there are some things in your life that you can't control. It's okay to feel your feelings and grieve about losing a job, but ruminating on it ultimately isn't productive. The best thing you can do for yourself in this situation is accept your unemployment and move on. Once you're able to do this, you'll be able to search for a new job and get your life back on track.

SEGUE

Life is full of unique challenges, and many of these challenges — particularly money problems, job loss, illness diagnosis, and grief — can trigger anxiety in a lot of people. Existing as a human being is difficult, but it's also beautiful. You have the power to be responsible for your own happiness and health, even when life throws you curveballs. In the next chapter, I'll discuss some of the anxiety triggers you may face in your everyday life — as well as some strategies to help you cope with these triggers.

4

TRIGGER 2: WHEN LIFE JUST HAPPENS...

"He who is not every day conquering some fear has not learned the secret of life."

— RALPH WALDO EMERSON

While big life challenges, like losing a job or getting a serious health diagnosis, are almost always anxiety-inducing, there are a number of everyday life challenges that can be quite triggering for people with anxiety as well. Big anxiety triggers — like going to college or starting a new job — can branch off into a whole bunch of smaller triggers, such as having to live with a roommate for the first time or having to give a presentation at work. While these changes are exciting, they can also be quite nerve-wracking, especially for someone with an anxiety disorder. For some, the anxiety might outweigh the excitement, which may ruin the mood and prevent the anxiety sufferer from enjoying what should be an invigorating time in their life.

When Charles was a freshman in college, he found it nearly impossible to leave his dorm room for the first few weeks. Even going to the cafeteria felt like too much because of his social anxiety. He started spending money he didn't have on microwaveable meals and takeout just so he could avoid going to the cafeteria — where he was sure he'd be forced to sit alone around hundreds of people — which in his mind, was the absolute *worst*. Of course, this was his heightened sense of anxiety attempting to protect him from social rejection. His anxiety convinced him that it was better to be alone all by himself than to sit alone while surrounded by a bunch of strangers.

The problem with this logic is, if you never put yourself out there, strangers will continue to be strangers. Charles was introverted to an extreme, but he eventually realized that he was going to have to rip the bandaid off and make some friends. He started talking casually with people in his classes, and joined his school's rowing team, which made him feel like a part of a community. Suddenly, he had people to sit with in the cafeteria and friends to hang out with on the weekends. Making friends can take time for people with anxiety, but it's totally possible and completely worth it.

Let's talk more about the anxiety triggers that often come with going to college, as well as some other notable everyday life changes that may heavily impact people with anxiety issues — such as being a new parent, starting a new job, and dealing with family and relationship problems. I'll also go over some coping strategies you can use to manage your anxiety in specific situations.

COLLEGE

College is an exciting time for most people because it offers students the ability to live independently, make new friends, and explore new ideas — even in the midst of the hustle and bustle of final exams and graduation celebrations. These changes can oftentimes be challenging for college students, as well as high school students and parents who are thinking ahead. College students abruptly cut themselves off from their usual community of friends and family overnight, which can understandably be very stressful. At the same time, they have to learn how to manage a hefty workload, live with roommates, and establish an individual identity. It's no wonder that college students are so anxious!

If you're going to college soon, you might have some concerns about what's to come. This anxiety you're feeling is totally normal, but that doesn't mean it's easy to deal with. It might help to define and pinpoint your specific anxieties regarding college, so we'll delve into that next as well as go over some effective coping mechanisms you can use to make your college stress a little more manageable.

What It Can Feel Like

Going to college can be scary — for students and parents alike. It's a whole new world, and as a student, you're being separated from your friends, family, and everything you know (usually for the first time). As a new college student, you might be concerned about living with a roommate and making new friends. You might wonder how you're going to manage your work-load, because it's likely going to be heavier than it was in high school. College is also a time for self-discovery. This can be daunting for people with anxiety, but it can also be super exciting! You'll be independent from your parents and your hometown for the first time. It's the perfect opportunity to work on yourself and discover who you are as a person.

What It Can Look Like

New college students will frequently experience homesickness, which is actually a form of separation anxiety. Chances are you've been homesick before. Maybe you missed your parents while at sleep-away camp when you were a kid, or perhaps you spent a week at your grandparents' house across the country and couldn't get over the feeling of wanting to go home. Homesickness is a common stress response for most new college students, especially those who are more introverted. The symptoms of homesickness in college students may include nausea, loss of appetite, trouble sleeping, shaking or trembling, muscle tension, fatigue, and struggling to pay attention and sit still while in class.

As an anxious college student, you may have trouble speaking up during lectures. Test-taking might be difficult for you, especially if you have anxiety in conjunction with ADHD (which is fairly common). You might struggle to turn in assignments on time, and, like Charles, you might keep to yourself and isolate in your dorm room rather than socialize with other students. You may begin to feel out of control, and like you just want to go home. These feelings are normal, but they can also be incredibly overwhelming. My advice is to stick with it. No matter how much you're struggling, things will get better with time. If you're really unhappy at your college, transferring schools is always an option as well.

What Can You Do?

If you're a college student who's currently struggling with anxiety, there are a number of things you can do to help yourself feel better. The strategies listed below should help you quell your homesickness as well as be the best student you can be — both academically and socially. Keep in mind that it may take some time to find your niche and your people in college, but when you do, you'll forget that you were ever homesick in the first place.

Keep a Normal Routine

As human beings, we thrive on routine. When you were in high school, you probably had a daily routine that worked quite well for you. Now that you're in college, you get to figure out a brand new daily routine for yourself. Make sure to keep your calendar updated with your class schedule. I used a whiteboard calendar, and hung it up next to my bed in my dorm room. I can't recommend this enough! Try not to overload yourself with schoolwork, as college isn't *just* about academics.

Make time for friends, clubs, sports, or whatever else you're interested in.

Watch Your Nutrition and Diet

Although living on pizza and instant ramen may be tempting, this type of diet isn't very good for your brain and body. Your school's dining hall may be relatively lackluster, but chances are, it at least has a salad bar. If you're on a meal plan — most college freshmen are — you shouldn't have any trouble getting your daily dose of proteins, carbs, fruits, and vegetables. I'm not saying you should deny yourself the occasional treat every once in a while. Just don't go overboard with it. Maintain a healthy diet, and your brain and body will be happy.

Take Breaks

College students are prone to overworking themselves. This is especially true for students in STEM, although writing a 10-12 page literature paper is no walk in the park either. Remember to be realistic about your course load (especially as a freshman), and don't forget to take breaks every once in a while. For people with anxiety and ADHD, the Pomodoro technique can work wonders. Setting a Pomodoro timer will allow you to focus on your work for 25-minute increments while taking short breaks in between. It's a truly fantastic way to study. While taking breaks from studying, try going for a walk around campus or call up an old friend from home. You'll be able to return to your assignment feeling refreshed and ready to work.

Find Resources on Campus

You'll have a difficult time finding a college campus that doesn't have a mental health resource center. If you've been struggling with anxiety, depression, or homesickness, don't be afraid to ask for help. You should be able to see a counselor on campus for relatively cheap as often as you need to. A good counselor will be able to help you organize your thoughts and take some of the emotional weight you've been feeling off your shoulders.

BEING A NEW PARENT

This might feel like a bit of a jump, but hey — there are few things more stressful than being a new parent. Now that we've talked about some of the stressors that can trigger anxiety in college students, let's discuss the most anxiety-inducing parts of having a baby and being a parent for the first time. Like going to college, having a baby is a major milestone. Your whole life changes after you have a baby, which can send some new parents into a state of shock. New mothers in particular might experience postpartum depression (or post-partum anxiety, which isn't talked about quite as much).

Postpartum anxiety can be just as debilitating as post-partum depression. Most of the time, they go hand-in-hand. It's definitely not something that should be ignored or brushed aside. Postpartum anxiety symp-toms generally take the form of intense worry, in contrast to postpartum depression, which can make new parents feel extremely depressed or even disinter-ested in their baby. The author of *The Hormone Cure*, Sara Gottfried, M.D., claims that you continuously feel nervous and tense while experiencing postpartum anxi-ety. "I think of postpartum anxiety as the loss of a normal sense of balance and calm, and postpartum depression as a loss of heart," she states. Let's discuss what postpartum anxiety can feel like below, as that should help you gain a deeper understanding of it.

What It Can Feel Like

Those who are suffering from postpartum anxiety will typically go through bouts of insomnia due to their intense anxious feelings. Basically, they're plagued by the fear that their baby will stop breathing in their sleep, even if the baby is perfectly healthy. If you have postpartum anxiety, you might be afraid to leave your baby alone for a few minutes with an adult you trust —

even your spouse. Sometimes, postpartum anxiety can ignite acute agoraphobia in new parents. You might be afraid to leave your house due to the fear of someone hurting you or your baby. You might spend a lot of time worrying about the worst-case scenarios — so much so that you won't be able to enjoy all of the wonderful parts of being a new parent.

What It Can Look Like

If you've been diagnosed with postpartum anxiety, you may experience physical symptoms, such as nausea, loss of appetite, and shortness of breath. You might avoid certain people and activities, or have trouble relaxing and sitting still. Some postpartum anxiety sufferers will get into the habit of checking things over and over again (which is a symptom that is oftentimes related to OCD). Usually, this stems from the tendency to be overly cautious, even in situations that aren't danger-ous. You're more likely to experience postpartum anxiety if you have a history of it in your family, or if your hormones are fluctuating a lot — which tends to happen to most mothers shortly after giving birth.

What Can You Do?

If you're having a hard time with being a new parent, you're definitely not alone. Being a new parent is *hard* work, and it makes sense that you'd feel anxious (and exhausted) from time to time. If you're suffering from postpartum depression or postpartum anxiety, being a new parent can be even more challenging. Here are a few things you can do if you're struggling during those first few months of parenthood.

Cuddle Your Baby

Cuddling with your baby is a great way to bond with them. Spend enough time cuddling and holding your baby, and you might just find that this activity is beneficial for both of you. When you cuddle your baby, your brain releases oxytocin. This can significantly reduce your anxiety, as well as make your baby feel loved and safe. (Pro tip: Try smelling the top of your newborn's head when you're feeling particularly anxious. This smell is usually quite pleasant and can be incredibly comforting for new parents).

Develop a Support System

Raising a new baby is hard, but you don't have to do it alone. Hopefully, you have a supportive partner and family members who are willing to help out once in a while. Trust me — your mom wants nothing more than to love and spoil your little one. That's what grandmas are for! There are also plenty of online support groups for new parents who are struggling, so if you're a single parent and you don't live close to your parents, that might be something to look into.

Take Care of Yourself

New parents have a tendency to forget about their own needs and focus solely on the needs of their baby. While taking care of your baby is important, you should also make sure that your own needs are being met. Try to maintain a healthy diet, and sleep as much as you can. It may be a little rough for those first few months, but it will get easier! Just keep trucking along.

FAMILY/SIGNIFICANT OTHER

There's a reason the holidays are such a stressful time for most people, and that reason is — unfortunately — family. Now, I love my family, but there's no denying that they can be a little much at times. Perhaps you feel the same way. Being around one's parents (and extended family in particular) can be anxiety-inducing for adults who have been living on their own for a long time. When you bring your significant other into the mix, it can make the situation all the more stressful.

You might be concerned about how your family will treat your significant other, or you might worry that your partner won't like your family.

What It Can Feel Like

People with anxiety are typically afraid of conflict, so it makes sense that reuniting with family members you've had conflicts with in the past would ignite some anxious feelings within you. Young adults who aren't following in their parents' footsteps (i.e. perhaps you became an artist instead of a doctor) might feel pressured by their parents to pursue a different career path. This can be frustrating, invalidating, and very, very anxiety-inducing — but remember: you're an adult and you get to be your own person.

It's also common for young adults with anxiety to dread the questions their parents are going to ask them or their significant other at the dinner table. Nobody wants to feel like they're being interviewed over Thanksgiving dinner, after all. Try to keep in mind that you don't have to answer any questions you don't want to answer. Your parents are only asking these questions because they love and care about you, but you're allowed to tell them if they're being too nosy!

What It Can Look Like

People with anxiety disorders might find themselves reverting back to child-like behavior when they're forced to spend more time than they're accustomed to spending with their parents and siblings. You might find yourself throwing tantrums or arguing with your sister, like you did when you were a teenager. While this can be an alarming experience, it's quite normal, and it stems from anxiety. This holiday season, try to be aware of your own behavior, and in the face of conflict, try to be the bigger person. This should help you to feel less anxious.

What Can You Do?

There are a number of things you can do to quell your anxious feelings when you're spending time with family. One of the best things you can do is anticipate any potential triggers. If you know that your mom is going to start asking you questions about work, for example, you can decide ahead of time how you're going to respond to those questions. You should also try to keep comforting people (and pets!) close by. If your partner is your rock, then stick by them and confide in them when your family is making you feel anxious or depressed. Hugging your dog once in a while can't hurt, either!

Try to stay grounded in the present, and don't take anything that your parents or siblings say personally. It's also important that you speak up for yourself when a family member has hurt your feelings. Sometimes, our loved ones hurt us without even realizing it. Speaking up for yourself may be a great way to prevent a certain family member from sticking their foot in their mouth again. It's also a good idea to set some boundaries if your family members are particularly nosy. For example, your parents have got to keep in mind that you're an adult now, and they can't just barge into the bedroom that you and your partner are sharing while you're there.

WORK

Ah, yes... work. Is there any daily activity that's more stressful than work? Feeling concerned, anxious, uncomfortable, or tense about one's job or one's relationships with coworkers is often referred to as workplace anxiety. Anxiety at work is widespread; studies show that over 40% of Americans say they experience workplace stress on the daily. While a little bit of stress at work is normal, excessive workplace anxiety can have a detrimental impact on your mental health and physical well-being. This may cause issues in both your personal and professional lives if you don't know how to cope with it.

What It Can Feel Like

Granted, when it comes to work, there are usually a lot of things to be stressed out about. Depending on the type of job you have, you might have to talk on the phone a lot or interact with customers who don't seem to understand basic human decency. I worked in food service throughout my twenties, so trust me — I get it. People with workplace anxiety will often worry about things like driving to work, making small talk with their colleagues, giving presentations, and speaking up in meetings. Some may stress out about finances if their job doesn't pay them enough. Most minimum-wage employees have to take a second job or a side gig to afford the cost of living these days, which only adds to their workplace anxiety.

What It Can Look Like

Those who are struggling with workplace anxiety may fail to meet deadlines or take too long to complete tasks they would normally have no trouble completing. If you have anxiety at work, you might have a difficult time concentrating during meetings and interactions with customers. You may start taking more sick days to avoid going to work, or you may develop some somatic symptoms — such as headaches, dizziness, and an upset stomach. People with workplace anxiety tend to get burnt out more quickly than people who don't suffer from this type of anxiety. This burnt-out feeling can spill over into your personal life, and affect your non-work-related relationships.

What Can You Do?

If you're currently suffering from workplace anxiety, you should know that you're not alone and that this feeling won't last forever. It's very important that you acknowledge your stressed-out feelings and talk to someone you trust about what you're going through. If you have a good manager, they can be a good support system for you, as can a friendly coworker. Remember to take breaks while at work. When I was working a particularly stressful job, I always found it helpful to put on my headphones and take a quick walk around the block. It's also important to know your limits and work within those limits. The number one thing that causes burnout and workplace anxiety is working too much, so just keep that in mind.

SEGUE

Keeping track of the things that trigger your anxiety on a daily basis can be incredibly helpful, as can utilizing the various coping mechanisms outlined in this chapter. In the next section, I'll dive into anxiety triggers that typically stem from trauma — such as the trauma we maintain from childhood or past relationships.

5

TRIGGER 3: WHEN THINGS GET PERSONAL...

66 *"In order to move on, you must understand why you felt what you did and why you no longer need to feel it."*

— MITCH ALBOM

For many people, their anxiety stems from past trauma, mostly (but not always) from childhood. The events that happen to you during your childhood are essentially the building blocks that make up the foundation for your adulthood. These events don't define who you are, but they *happened* — and the sooner you're able to accept that they happened, the sooner you'll be able to let go and live your adult life without these unfortunate events looming over you. This is easier said than done, but it isn't something you have to conquer on your own.

The fact of the matter is, if your childhood trauma is the main thing that's been triggering your adult anxiety (as is the case for many people), then something must be done about it. Thankfully, there are plenty of coping strategies you can use to help yourself in situations where your anxiety is getting triggered due to past traumatic experiences. One of the most effective ways to process childhood trauma is to participate in Cognitive Behavioral Therapy. CBT is one of the best PTSD treatments out there, and considering the fact that anxiety tends to go hand-in-hand with PTSD, it's no surprise that CBT has been proven to help anxiety patients with trauma-related anxiety triggers.

A friend of mine (who I'll call "Maddy") gave me permission to share the following story with you. When Maddy was a little girl, she had a difficult home life. You would never guess that this was the case because she went to school with a smile every day and was generally very curious about the world. Little did her teachers and classmates know, her parents got into screaming matches almost every night. Her father was an alcoholic, and he would oftentimes lash out at Maddy when she tried to stand up for her mother.

Her mother eventually became emotionally unavailable and distant towards her, despite Maddy's efforts to help her. Of course, Maddy should never have been put in that position in the first place. She was only nine years old. She started developing symptoms of anxiety and PTSD, like insomnia and nightmares. She had trouble eating and began to have panic attacks at school on a regular basis. Her dad, at this point, was too far gone, and her mom dismissed her symptoms as being overly sensitive.

When Maddy turned ten, her dad left in the middle of the night and never came back. This meant that Maddy's mom had to raise her on her own. Although both of them felt some relief after Maddy's dad left, Maddy's mom was struggling to make ends meet. She started taking double shifts at work, which meant Maddy was left alone for hours at a time. She began to feel lonely and sad, and with no one to share her worries with, she eventually started self-harming.

After a few months, Maddy's mother noticed the scars covering her daughter's arms. She decided to take Maddy to a therapist, who — after years of Cognitive Behavioral Therapy — helped Maddy understand the ways in which her traumatic past impacted her mental health. By the time she was sixteen, Maddy learned how to utilize certain coping strategies, such as mindfulness and journaling. She also learned how to express her thoughts and emotions, which allowed her to begin to heal from the trauma she'd experienced.

As Maddy grew older, she gained confidence and independence. She excelled in school, made new friends, and even landed her dream job as a wildlife conservationist. She learned how to recognize and cope with her anxiety triggers — which included things like men yelling and children crying. She also learned how to set necessary boundaries with those who had hurt her in the past, which allowed her to prioritize her mental health.

Despite going through trauma during her childhood, Maddy was eventually able to overcome her anxiety and thrive as an adult. It wasn't easy, and it admittedly took some time, but going through this healing process was absolutely crucial to her adult happiness. Her past trauma had been preventing her from living her life to the fullest, and she didn't want that to be the case forever.

If you're struggling with anxiety triggers brought on by past trauma, you're definitely not alone. In this chapter, we'll discuss both childhood trauma and relationship trauma as significantly impactful anxiety triggers. Let's take a closer look at what these past traumas can look and feel like, as well as go over some coping strategies you can use to quell your anxious feelings after you've been triggered.

This may be a difficult chapter for some people, so feel free to skip it now and come back to it when you're ready. Being uncomfortable is a big part of the healing process, but you shouldn't have to be uncomfortable until you're ready to be uncomfortable. Just keep that in mind. Without further ado, let's get into it, shall we?

(CHILDHOOD) TRAUMA

Experiencing childhood trauma can certainly increase one's risk of developing anxiety disorders, like PTSD, OCD, and Social Anxiety Disorder. As I mentioned previously, the best way to address your feelings of anxiety — once you've been triggered — is to confront your trauma directly. It's also important to remember that anxiety is a common condition, so you're not going through this alone. As we've already learned, anxiety can manifest in several different forms, such as persistent and intense worry about everyday situations. Those who have been through childhood trauma are statistically more likely to experience these types of symptoms, which can sometimes lead to the development of an anxiety disorder.

Childhood trauma is a well-known phenomenon, and it's something that can stay with us throughout our lives. Oftentimes, childhood trauma can cause anxiety that we may not even realize is rooted in past experiences. Even when we do recognize the source of our trauma, it can be difficult to deal with and move past for most people. The reason childhood trauma tends to linger is that we often suppress it, which tends to manifest as PTSD over time. It's a natural tendency to avoid painful situations, but burying your problems is ultimately more harmful than it is helpful.

Your childhood experiences, both good and bad, have shaped who you are today. The people you were surrounded by as a kid (i.e. family, friends, teachers, and strangers) have all impacted you in different ways. Unfortunately, as children, it's not uncommon for us to be hurt by the adults in our lives — which can lead to a general feeling of distrust in those who suffer from anxiety and PTSD. It's important to recognize that exploring issues like anxiety will usually involve looking back at your past experiences. You've got to acknowledge and address your past traumas in order to effectively move forward and heal.

What It Can Feel Like

Childhood trauma-based anxiety is a complicated problem, and it's not something that's easy for most people to deal with. The thing about childhood trauma-based anxiety is, you never really know how it's going to manifest. Some people might feel like they're worrying all the time, even if things aren't actually that bad. Others might be on edge and unable to relax, or feel restless a lot of the time. Emotions can be intense and unpredictable, making it hard to feel like you're in control. It's also pretty common to feel like you're always on guard, and those with PTSD might have repetitive dreams or memories that are especially distressing.

Unfortunately, some people turn to drugs or alcohol to help deal with all of these feelings, which can make matters worse. On top of that, it can be really hard to concentrate, or to stop thinking about all the worst possible outcomes of any given situation. Making decisions is particularly difficult when you're dealing with this kind of anxiety, because it feels like there's always something to worry about. Letting go of your worries can be almost impossible, and some may feel like they'll be stuck with their worries for the rest of their life. This, in a nutshell, is what childhood trauma-based anxiety can feel like.

What It Can Look Like

Again, there's no telling how childhood trauma-based anxiety is going to manifest. It typically depends on the person and the experiences they've been through. That said, this type of anxiety might make it particularly difficult for you to fall asleep, which means you might be exhausted during the day a lot of the time. You might notice concerning changes in your behavior, or feel like your thoughts are out of control.

It's also not uncommon for people with childhood trauma-based anxiety to experience physical symptoms — such as muscle tension, twitchiness, and extreme sensitivity to one's environment. Everyday situations might feel like too much to handle, and you may feel especially jumpy in situations that are somewhat triggering (even if that particular situation is not, in and of itself, dangerous). Due to constantly being on edge, you may occasionally feel sick to your stomach. You might feel like you're being watched or overanalyze other people's reactions to certain situations. These feelings and symptoms can be difficult to deal with, and they can ultimately take a significant toll on your relationships with others.

What Can You Do?

If you're struggling with anxiety that stems from childhood trauma, there are thankfully a number of things you can do to help yourself feel better. My friend, Maddy, probably would have had a much harder time dealing with her anxiety had she not gotten serious about doing what was necessary to heal after going through trauma. Let's go over some of the most effective coping strategies that I came across in my research below.

Cognitive Behavioral Therapy (CBT)

In trauma-based Cognitive Behavioral Therapy, a therapist helps you recognize your negative thought patterns that are related to the traumatic events you've experienced and challenges them. They help you understand that these thoughts are unproductive and that they're negatively impacting your well-being and personal relationships. In CBT, you work with the therapist on replacing your harmful thought patterns with more positive and realistic ones. This process takes time and patience, but it can eventually help you heal and move forward, so it's definitely worth it.

Prolonged Exposure (PE) Therapy

This type of therapy can be very helpful for people with severe PTSD. The idea behind PE is to gradually expose the anxiety patient to their traumatic memories and experiences in a safe and controlled environment. Over time, this exposure can help to reduce the fear and anxiety the person associates with these memories, which will eventually allow them to process and come to terms with what happened during their childhood. PE is often used in conjunction with other forms of therapy, such as CBT, to provide a more effective approach to treating childhood trauma-based anxiety.

Face Your Feelings

When it comes to coping with childhood trauma-based anxiety, facing your feelings head-on can be daunting. However, it's a necessary step toward healing. It can be tempting to push painful emotions aside or bury them deep down, but the truth is that these feelings will only continue to fester if you bottle them up. By acknowledging and allowing yourself to feel your emotions, you can begin to process and work through them in a healthy way. Although it may be difficult at first, it will ultimately be well worth it.

Prioritize Self-Care

Needless to say, trauma can take a huge toll on both your mental and physical health. For this reason, it's important that you make time for self-care activities as they can help you feel more grounded. Self-care can include meditation, journaling, physical exercise, spending time in nature, or simply taking a few minutes to breathe and check in with yourself. It's also important to note that a big part of self-care is setting boundaries and learning to say no to things you don't want to do.

Medication

Medication isn't always necessary, but it can be exceptionally helpful for some people who are struggling with extreme trauma-based anxiety. Talk with your therapist or healthcare provider about going on anti-anxiety or antidepressant medication if you feel like it might benefit you. Although there's some stigma surrounding using medication to treat mental health disorders, it's exceedingly common and is nothing to be ashamed of. Medication is typically used in tandem with CBT and Prolonged Exposure Therapy. Personally, I would only use this tactic as a last resort once you put the work in with other non-medicated therapies.

PAST ROMANTIC RELATIONSHIPS

Now that we've discussed the ins and outs of childhood trauma-based anxiety, let's move on to a different type of anxiety trigger — trauma that stems from past romantic relationships. Have you ever felt doubts, insecurities, and a constant need for reassurance in a relationship, even when everything seems perfect? This is what's known as relationship anxiety. Relationship anxiety is a surprisingly common experience, and it can often stem from early childhood trauma. It usually indicates an insecure attachment style and severe abandonment or trust issues in people who suffer from this type of anxiety, however, that's not always the case.

For a person with relationship anxiety, questions like "Do they really like me?" and "How long until this falls apart?" can plague their thoughts, even if they've already exchanged "I love yous" with their partner. While it's normal to have some worries about a relationship, extreme anxiety can significantly impact its growth or even prevent a relationship from starting altogether. Let's take a closer look at how relationship anxiety can manifest, as well as what you can do to more effectively cope with your trauma from past relationships.

What It Can Feel Like

For those who suffer from relationship anxiety, it can feel all-consuming. This type of anxiety tends to take a major toll on your emotional well-being as well as your romantic relationships. It's like having a never-ending barrage of questions bombarding your mind — making you constantly question yourself, your partner, and the relationship as a whole. You might find yourself wondering whether or not you truly matter to your partner, or worry about the possibility of a breakup. You may frequently ask your partner for reassurance or validation, which can put a strain on your relationship.

Relationship anxiety may also lead you to doubt the long-term compatibility of your relationship, which could leave you feeling uneasy and uncertain about your future with your partner. These feelings can make it difficult for people with this type of anxiety to truly enjoy their romantic relationships, which is a saddening issue. Love is one of the best experiences in the world, and it's not fair that your anxiety is preventing you from fully experiencing all of the beauty that comes with it.

Retrospective Jealousy

Have you ever felt uncomfortable or insecure when thinking about a romantic partner's past relationships or experiences? It's normal to feel a bit insecure about these kinds of things, but if it gets to the point of obsession, you might want to consider talking to a therapist about whether or not you could have relationship anxiety. This type of jealousy can be particularly difficult for anxious people to deal with because it's based on events that have already happened and cannot be changed.

That said, it's important to remember that your past relationships and experiences are a part of who you are. You might not be happy about some of your partner's past relationship choices, but at least they've been honest with you about those choices. The best thing you can do for yourself is focus on the present and the future of your relationship with this person, rather than dwell on the past. Communication and trust are key when it comes to overcoming retrospective jealousy and building a strong, healthy relationship.

What It Can Look Like

Relationship anxiety affects everyone differently. However, some symptoms you can typically expect to come across include feeling unmotivated, tired, and emotionally drained. To make matters worse, these symptoms can also cause physical discomfort, like upset stomachs and headaches. People with relationship anxiety have a tendency to accidentally mess things up by starting arguments with their partner or by distancing themselves even though they're really upset. This could manifest in different ways, like hanging out with a toxic ex or overanalyzing their partner's words or actions.

People with relationship anxiety usually need a lot of reassurance from their partner. They might always want to be around their partner and be somewhat clingy, which could cause them to act a bit controlling at times. Some people with relationship anxiety might give their partner the silent treatment for the sake of avoiding conflict — or, they might do things to please their partner, even if it means giving up what they want.

There are plenty of reasons why someone might develop relationship anxiety. Perhaps they had a partner who cheated on them in the past, or maybe their first love broke up with them out of the blue. Other factors, such as low self-esteem, an insecure attachment style, or a tendency to doubt their partner's feelings can also contribute to relationship anxiety.

What Can You Do?

Thankfully, if you're suffering from relationship anxiety, there are certain actions you can take to help remedy the issue. One option that experts recommend for treating and managing relationship anxiety is couples therapy, which may include attending psychoeducational sessions with your partner. Let's go over some of the most effective coping strategies when it comes to overcoming relationship anxiety below.

Maintain Your Identity

As you and your partner get closer, you may begin to notice that some aspects of your identity or independence have started to shift in order to make space for the relationship. This is a common occurrence as couples become more intertwined. While certain adjustments, like adjusting to your partner's sleep schedule, may not affect your sense of self, others might have a more significant impact. It's important that you maintain a sense of self in every relationship you enter into. You shouldn't change yourself solely to please your partner, as this won't benefit either of you in the long run. It's very important that you communicate with your partner and find ways to compromise and grow together while still maintaining both of your individual identities.

Confront Your Anxiety

Charles and Maddy got where they are today because they learned how to confront their anxiety head-on. If you're having trouble confronting your relationship anxiety, a therapist should be able to help you do so. They should also be able to help you get used to normalizing feelings of jealousy. It's crucial to recognize that while these feelings are valid, they're not always logical.

Practice Good Communication

If you're struggling with anxiety in your relationship, it's absolutely essential that you have honest and open conversations with your partner about your worries and expectations for the future. Share any doubts you may have with them, and work through any challenges together. This will ultimately be much better than inventing worst-case scenarios in your head and getting angry with your partner for no reason they'll be able to understand.

Cognitive Behavioral Conjoint Therapy

Cognitive Behavioral Conjoint Therapy (CBCT) is a type of therapy that can help couples work through relationship anxiety. This type of therapy focuses specifically on identifying and changing negative thought patterns and behaviors that can cause anxiety and stress in a relationship. CBCT can help couples learn how to communicate more effectively with one another, as well as develop better problem-solving skills. With the guidance of a trained therapist, you and your partner will be able to learn how to relate to each other in new ways. This should eventually help you develop a healthier, more satisfying relationship.

Enjoy the Present

When it comes to being in a romantic relationship, there's nothing better than living in the moment. Focusing on the present moment can be an especially effective way to cope with relationship anxiety — especially for those with anxiety disorders. By enjoying the present, you'll be able to redirect your attention away from your worries and instead focus on living your best life with your partner. If you're having trouble enjoying the present, try doing fun activities with your partner — such as going for walks or cooking together. You should also put effort into being mindful of your thoughts and behaviors, as this will help you to become more attuned to your own emotions as well as those of your partner.

SEGUE

It can be especially difficult to face the anxiety triggers that stem from particularly personal issues — such as childhood trauma or problems you've had to deal with in past romantic relationships. However, confronting these triggers is a necessary part of healing and over-coming your anxiety in the long run. If you're struggling, consider meeting with a Cognitive Behavioral Therapist. Prioritize self-care and do your best to enjoy the present moment. In the next section, I'll dive a little deeper into social anxiety and the actions you can take to more effectively cope with it.

6

TRIGGER 4: WHEN GET-TOGETHERS MAKE YOU FALL APART...

> *"You wouldn't worry so much about what others think of you if you realized how seldom they do."*

— ELEANOR ROOSEVELT

Social anxiety can be a particularly difficult beast to tame. It's surprising how common social anxiety is, however, there's some confusion surrounding it because it's often misread as introversion — which may slightly overlap with social anxiety, but it's ultimately not the same thing. Unlike run-of-the-mill introversion, social anxiety can be an overwhelming and paralyzing experience for a lot of people. The mere thought of being in a crowded room or making small talk with a group of strangers can trigger a flood of uncomfortable emotions and physical sensations for people who struggle with social anxiety.

Some people with this type of anxiety may experience symptoms like sweaty palms, increased heart rate, racing thoughts, and an upset stomach. It can make it very difficult to be around other people, and not just in the context of parties and get-togethers. Even just going to the grocery store can feel like an insurmountable task for someone with social anxiety.

Social anxiety is oftentimes deeply rooted in the fear of being judged or rejected — which may or may not stem from past trauma for some people. This fear can lead those with social anxiety to avoid social situations altogether. Take Charles, for instance. When he was in his mid-twenties, he seldom went to get-togethers with his friends because his social anxiety was so bad. He always seemed to have an excuse for why he couldn't make it to this and that get-together. "I'm too tired," he'd tell us. "I have to be up early tomorrow," etc., etc.

Some people in our friend group began to wonder if Charles didn't like hanging out with them. They became concerned and eventually annoyed that he never seemed to want to spend any time with them. Little did they know, Charles would have loved to get together with us to see a movie or go out for drinks. It was just that he was under the control of his social anxiety. Charles was aware that some people in our friend group were irritated with him, too, which only made his anxiety worse. (There's a lesson in here about being patient with your friends who struggle with social anxiety. They *want* to spend time with you, but their anxiety makes it very difficult for them to do so.)

Eventually, Charles started talking to a therapist about his social anxiety. She taught him about some techniques and strategies he could use to more effectively cope with being anxious in public. He learned how to talk back to his negative thoughts, and after a while, was able to reframe them completely. He realized that catastrophizing and ruminating about being judged by his friends was ultimately unhelpful and unproductive. It took some time for him to reframe his anxious thoughts into more productive ones, but it was time well-spent. I think he'd definitely agree that it was worth it.

Although Charles is doing much better now, he still has to work extra hard to be fully present in social situations. He practices mindful breathing before and during get-togethers in order to avoid letting his social anxiety get the best of him. Some days are more difficult than others, but he's learned to be patient with himself — and his friends who previously misunderstood what he was going through have learned to be patient with him as well.

It's important to keep in mind that overcoming social anxiety is a marathon, not a sprint. Like Charles, you might experience some especially hard days here and there, even after you've put the work in to properly address your social anxiety. When the going gets tough, remember to breathe and have compassion for yourself. Coping with social anxiety isn't easy, but it's definitely possible if you're willing to put the time and effort in.

In this chapter, we'll do a deep dive into social anxiety. Social anxiety is oftentimes misunderstood. There's a lot of misinformation out there — which can make things worse for socially anxious people who can't stop themselves from Googling the symptoms. I want to use this opportunity to clear some things up. What *is* social anxiety, exactly? What are the most common root causes of this unique type of anxiety, and what sort of daily activities tend to trigger it? We'll go over all of this and more in this chapter, so if you've been struggling with social anxiety, don't fret! Taking back your life is totally possible, just as long as you have the right information and tools on hand.

WHAT IS SOCIAL ANXIETY?

Social anxiety disorder is an extremely common form of anxiety that many people struggle with. In other words, if you're currently battling social anxiety, you're not alone. This debilitating condition can make it difficult to engage in social situations, even with friends and other loved ones, especially if the socially anxious person feels judged or scrutinized in any way. A person with social anxiety may have difficulty speaking in public, going on dates, attending job interviews, or even just talking to a cashier at the grocery store. Simple tasks like eating or drinking in front of other people can trigger social anxiety for some, as they may fear being humiliated or rejected based on the way others perceive them.

The fear that comes with social anxiety disorder is often so intense that it feels impossible to control. For some people, it can prevent them from going to work or school. Others may be able to push through, but they'll still experience a lot of fear and anxiety, and be totally exhausted when they get home. It's not uncommon for people with this type of anxiety to worry about upcoming social situations for weeks in advance, and some may end up avoiding certain places or events altogether.

While some people with social anxiety disorder only experience anxious thoughts or symptoms during performances (i.e. giving speeches, playing music on stage, competing in sports, etc.), others may experience anxiety that gets triggered by any type of social interaction. Social anxiety disorder typically develops in late childhood and can oftentimes be misread as extreme shyness or introversion. Social anxiety disorder is also more common in women than in men, especially among teenagers and young adults. If left untreated, social anxiety disorder may last for several years (or even a lifetime for some).

COMMON ROOT CAUSES OF SOCIAL ANXIETY

Social anxiety is more complicated than most people realize. It can be caused by a lot of different factors, or, a combination of factors — including genetics, environmental issues, cognitive biases, and cultural influences. Genetics definitely plays a significant role in the development of social anxiety for some. Experts have identified the SLCGA4 (serotonin transporter) gene as a potential contributor to social anxiety. Those who have socially anxious parents are also more likely to develop social anxiety disorder. It basically has a lot to do with the effects of nature and nurture. Let's go over some of the most common root causes of social anxiety below.

Parental Shortcomings

You're unfortunately more likely to develop social anxiety if you grew up with parents who were overcontrolling, quick to criticize, reluctant to show affection, or overly concerned about the opinions of other people. Kids who grow up in these types of environments are at risk of developing an insecure attachment style, which can end up manifesting as social anxiety later in life. Older siblings who are burdened with the task of caring for their younger brothers and sisters when their parents aren't around are also at risk of developing social anxiety.

Social Trauma

When Charles was in high school, he got bullied relentlessly by this group of guys that just could not seem to leave him alone. This undoubtedly contributed to the social anxiety he experienced as an adult. Traumatic social experiences — like being bullied or teased by your peers — can definitely cause a person to develop social anxiety disorder. Witnessing other people's traumatic social experiences can also lead to the development of this disorder, especially if you've been through the trauma you're witnessing yourself.

Lack of Social Skills

While some people are natural social butterflies, others just aren't — which is perfectly okay. Factors like introversion, ADHD, and Autism can sometimes play a role in a person's lack of social skills, but this isn't always the case. Sometimes, being social is just difficult. As an introvert, this is something I've come to understand quite well.

If you struggle to communicate effectively with others or have difficulties forming relationships in general, it may be because you have social anxiety. These struggles can also lead to the development of social anxiety. If you're not really sure what's going on with your brain, it might be a good idea to meet with a therapist. They should be able to provide you with some much-needed clarity, which will in turn help to quell your anxiety.

Cognitive Biases

Cognitive biases can have a profound impact on one's mental health. These biases refer to the unfavorable ways of thinking that can potentially lead some people to perceive themselves in a negative light. In short, cognitive biases are thought patterns that can distort a person's perceptions of reality. This means that someone with deeply-rooted cognitive biases might misinterpret certain social situations and interactions.

For example, a common cognitive bias that someone with social anxiety might experience is "catastrophic thinking." A person with the "catastrophic thinking" cognitive bias is basically hardwired to believe that the worst possible outcome will happen if they go to a certain social event, which is why people with social anxiety tend to avoid get-togethers with friends or coworkers. The negative thoughts and emotions that stem from this social avoidance can sometimes get so overwhelming that the socially anxious person might end up developing depression in conjunction with social anxiety.

Cultural Differences

Social anxiety is a universal phenomenon. Naturally, it can affect people across different cultures. However, the ways in which social anxiety manifests and the specific things that trigger it can vary depending on how a specific culture does things. For example, in individualistic cultures, such as the United States, socially anxious people may be triggered by the fear of not being perceived as independent or self-sufficient.

In collectivistic cultures, such as Japan, however, people with social anxiety might get triggered by the fear of not fitting in with a certain group or failing to meet group expectations.

Cultural differences in communication styles and social norms can also contribute to the development of social anxiety in some people. In many cultures, direct communication and assertiveness tend to be valued, while in others, indirect communication and avoidance of confrontation are preferred. This can oftentimes lead to confusion and anxiety for those who are not familiar with a certain culture's particular communication style.

SYMPTOMS OF SOCIAL ANXIETY

We've all been in situations where we feel nervous or uneasy around others. Maybe you've felt shy or anxious when meeting someone new or before giving a big presentation at work. Walking into a room full of strangers or speaking in public isn't everyone's cup of tea, but most people are able to manage it.

However, if you have social anxiety disorder, these situations can be too overwhelming to handle. You might start to avoid all social interactions because things that most people consider normal, like engaging in small talk or making eye contact while having a conversation, make you feel extremely uncomfortable. This can affect all aspects of your life, not just your social life — which could potentially lead to a mental breakdown if you ignore or brush aside your social anxiety for too long. Let's go over some of the symptoms that are most commonly associated with social anxiety below so that you can gain a deeper understanding of what you've been experiencing.

Emotional and Behavioral Symptoms

Social anxiety can cause a lot of emotional and behavioral symptoms, which can end up making simple tasks — like grocery shopping, or taking your dog for a walk in a busy park — exceptionally difficult. One of the most common symptoms people with social anxiety experience is the fear of being perceived in a negative light by other people. This fear can make a social situation, like a get-together, particularly stressful for a socially anxious person, as he may spend the entire evening panicking about whether or not he might embarrass himself.

As I've already briefly mentioned, people with social anxiety tend to avoid social events. They may isolate themselves in order to avoid potential embarrassment, and they're likely to feel uncomfortable when they're in a position where they're the center of attention (such as a surprise birthday party, for example). People with social anxiety may worry a lot before, during, and after social events. Some may even analyze their social performance after the fact, and beat themselves up if they feel like they didn't do well enough.

People with social anxiety also tend to have trouble making eye contact or speaking up when in social situations. These symptoms can make it exceptionally difficult for people with this affliction to form and maintain meaningful relationships with others, do well at work or in school, and enjoy all that life has to offer.

Physical Symptoms

Unsurprisingly, social anxiety doesn't come without some unpleasant physical symptoms as well. It can essentially make you feel like your body is betraying you. You might turn red as a tomato while talking to someone you have a crush on, or your hands might tremble uncontrollably while you're giving a presentation at work. In some situations, you may feel like you're going to puke your guts out. You might struggle to catch your breath at times, which can cause light-headedness and even fainting in rare cases.

You might find yourself crying a lot in situations where you feel overwhelmed, or you might feel like your mind has gone blank when someone asks you a question — even if you're an expert on whatever it is they're asking about. All of these physical symptoms can make social situations feel unbearable, but it's important to remember that you're not alone. If you've been experiencing any of the symptoms listed above, don't hesitate to reach out for help. There are plenty of ways to manage your social anxiety symptoms, and eventually overcome them — which we'll dive into next.

SOCIAL ANXIETY TRIGGERS

When it comes to managing social anxiety, identifying your triggers is the first necessary step you'll need to take. This may be easier said than done, especially considering the fact that a lot of different things can trigger social anxiety. It usually depends on the person and their past experiences, however, there are some common social anxiety triggers that you'll want to keep in mind.

Meeting New People

Walking into a room full of strangers is daunting for most people, but for those with social anxiety disorder, it can feel like an insurmountable task. The fear of being judged negatively by others can be incredibly overwhelming for some. If you have this particular fear, it may cause you to worry about potentially embarrassing or humiliating yourself in public. Even simple actions like maintaining eye contact or making small talk with a coworker can feel like scaling a mountain for those who suffer from social anxiety.

Dating

Dating can be a nerve-wracking experience, and for those with social anxiety disorder, it can feel like an impossible challenge. The thought of putting oneself out there, texting, making phone calls, and going on dates can be overwhelming — which may trigger symptoms of anxiety in some (or frankly most) people. It's important to keep in mind that for someone with social anxiety disorder, the fear of judgment and rejection can be paralyzing. They may worry that they won't measure up to their date's expectations, or that they'll embarrass themselves somehow. This fear can lead to certain behaviors that may confuse a socially anxious person's partner, such as canceling plans, declining date invitations, or even ghosting. Needless to say, this can inhibit a socially anxious person's ability to form romantic relationships.

Asking For Help From Customer Service Personnel

This is a big one. Despite the fact that customer service people are literally there to help you, you might find that you're unable to ask for the help you need if you suffer from social anxiety. I've been through a fair amount of social anxiety myself, and the fear of "annoying" a service worker with questions that may seem "stupid" or "obvious" is a very real thing. When I was in my early twenties, I didn't want to be perceived as annoying, so I avoided asking service workers for help. Similarly, I refused to send back incorrect meals or return things I'd purchased from the store that I was unsatisfied with — just because I didn't want to irritate the service workers. Remember, helping you is literally their job, so don't be afraid to ask for help when you need it.

Eating, Drinking, Reading, Writing, Typing... and Just Generally Existing in Front of Others

When you have social anxiety, everything you do can feel embarrassing — especially if there are other people around to perceive you, you know... living your life. It's important to keep in mind that everyone else is just trying to live their lives, too. In general, other people are too concerned with their own issues to even notice what you're doing in public. Nobody is going to judge you for reading, writing, eating, drinking, etc. in public because they're too busy worrying about being judged by other people for doing these exact things. Take a deep breath, and exist. Nobody is going to care that much about what you're doing in a public setting (as long as you're not streaking or running around yelling "purple hippo!" in people's faces). Just live your life! It's all going to be okay.

Being Teased

People with social anxiety tend to take being teased very personally. More often than not, those who suffer from social anxiety are Highly Sensitive People (HSP) which means they're extremely empathetic and may feel emotions on a deeper level than the average person. If you have social anxiety, you might not always pick up on the fact that a friend is teasing you. It's very easy for people with social anxiety to fall into a pit of negative thoughts, and teasing can sometimes trigger this.

Speaking on the Phone

There's a reason so many young people prefer texting over phone calls. Phone calls are anxiety-inducing! Older folks might prefer phone calls over texting because that's what they're used to, but the opposite is true for younger people. It can be especially difficult for people with social anxiety to talk on the phone with strangers or people they haven't talked to in a long time. This can make jobs where you have to cold call clients or deal with unsatisfied customers over the phone really difficult for those who have social anxiety.

WAYS TO COPE WITH SOCIAL ANXIETY

It's easy to feel helpless when it comes to the over-whelming symptoms of social anxiety disorder, but there are actually plenty of things you can do to help manage it. The first step is to change your mindset. People with social anxiety often have negative thoughts and beliefs that only further fuel their fears and anxi-eties. These negative thoughts may include:

"I'm sure I'll look like an idiot."
"My voice will start shaking, and everyone will
see how nervous I am."
"People will think I'm so boring and stupid."
"I won't know what to say, and everyone will see
how awkward I am."

Challenging these thoughts is an effective way to begin tackling your social anxiety symptoms. It's important to remind yourself that these are just thoughts, and your thoughts are not necessarily reality. Try to find evidence to refute your negative beliefs, and focus on the positive aspects when faced with a social situation. With time and practice, you can eventually change the way you think and overcome your social anxiety. Let's take a look at some coping strategies you can use to combat your social anxiety when you feel like you've been triggered.

Control Your Breathing

When anxiety takes hold, a cascade of physiological changes occurs in your body. Rapid breathing (or hyperventilation), for example, can disrupt the balance of oxygen and carbon dioxide within your system. This can end up triggering even more unpleasant physical symptoms — such as dizziness, a racing heart rate, and shortness of breath. The good news is, taking control of your breathing can help you regain balance in your body and alleviate some of these nasty physical symptoms. When practicing breath control, remember to sit comfortably and inhale slowly. Hold your breath for two seconds, exhale slowly, and repeat. Eventually, you'll notice yourself starting to feel better.

Face Your Fears

Facing your fears is key when it comes to coping with social anxiety, however, you don't want to bite off more than you can chew. Rather than attempting to face your biggest fear right away, try starting with something small. Perhaps you can strike up a conversation with a stranger at the grocery store, or invite your neighbor in for a cup of coffee sometime. If you have trouble with social interactions, training yourself to be more social can work wonders. It can alleviate your social fears and anxiety, which means you'll be able to lead a more fulfilling social life.

Try Progressive Muscle Relaxation

Progressive muscle relaxation is a technique that teaches you how to unwind your muscles when you're feeling stressed out. All you have to do is follow two simple steps. First, you tense up certain muscle groups like your neck and shoulders in the order that makes the most sense to you. Then, you let go of all that tightness and feel how your muscles loosen up. This exercise can be a lifesaver when you're feeling super anxious, as it can help you lower the tension levels in your body. It can even help with things like stomachaches,

132 | KIRK TEACHOUT

headaches, and insomnia — which is definitely a plus! Give it a try and see how it works for you.

Take the Focus Off of Yourself

Social anxiety tends to stem from insecurity and self-consciousness in social situations, typically due to past events and experiences. When you're in a nerve-wracking social situation, you should try to focus your attention on the people around you (but not on what they're thinking about you). Your anxiety isn't as visible as you think, so it's really not worth worrying about. Do your best to focus on and enjoy the present moment, or, in other words, don't let your anxiety hold you back from having a good time with your loved ones.

Challenge and Talk Back to Negative Thoughts

If you want to tackle your social anxiety at its core, you've got to challenge the negative thoughts that fuel it. This involves figuring out which thoughts trigger your anxiety or make you feel awkward in social situations, and questioning them. You also need to challenge the underlying beliefs (cognitive biases) that back up your negative thoughts. By doing so, you can start to reframe your thinking and talk back to your negative thoughts when they're getting you down.

Attend Cognitive Behavioral Therapy

Social anxiety disorder (and other anxiety disorders) can frequently be treated with cognitive behavioral therapy — which we've already touched on quite a bit. Studies show that cognitive behavioral therapy is a super effective way to treat social anxiety disorder, so it's definitely worth a shot. Cognitive behavioral therapy uses a combination of techniques, which essentially means you'll be tackling your social anxiety from all angles when you engage in CBT.

Medication

Certain medications, such as Benzodiazepines, antidepressants, and beta blockers, can be very helpful for those who are struggling with social anxiety. If you feel like medication might be helpful for you, talk to your therapist or doctor about your options. It's not necessarily a good idea to become too reliant on anti-anxiety medications, but they can be incredibly beneficial for those who need to get back on their feet after going through a breakdown.

SEGUE

Social anxiety is a unique beast, but if you have the right tools and know-how, you shouldn't have any trouble slaying it. Some common social anxiety triggers include meeting new people, asking for help, talking on the phone, and being teased. It's very important that you don't *avoid* these triggers, but *face* them instead. Confronting your social anxiety head-on is ultimately going to be what helps you overcome it in the long run. In the next chapter, I'll talk more about anxiety management techniques. This will include a couple of mindfulness exercises that you can try out on your own.

7

ANXIETY MANAGEMENT TECHNIQUES

66 *"You may not control all the events that happen to you, but you can decide not to be reduced by them."*

— MAYA ANGELOU

A nxiety simply isn't talked about enough due to the stigma that surrounds it. This definitely needs to change. How are people supposed to know how to manage their anxiety if no one ever broaches the subject? There are, thankfully, quite a lot of relaxation and mindfulness techniques out there that have gained popularity among people who struggle with anxiety — especially today. The fact that mindfulness has become so deeply integrated into a lot of people's daily routines, work lives, and sleep regimens is a sign that society is headed in the right direction in terms of taking anxiety disorders more seriously.

Charles is a pretty good example of someone who was afraid to get help for his anxiety issues because of the stigma he'd experienced and read about online. The thing was, Charles knew he needed help, but he'd heard way too many stories about people with anxiety losing their jobs or being labeled as "weak" or "crazy" by their friends and family members. He didn't want to be judged or ostracized by the people he loved, so he kept his feelings bottled up — which, of course, only made things worse.

His anxiety started to affect his job, as well as his relationship with his girlfriend. He began to isolate himself from his friends and refused to attend social gatherings because the thought alone made him sick with worry. After a certain point, he realized that he couldn't keep living like this. It was simply too much to handle. That was the day that he decided to take the first step toward getting help for his anxiety.

As he walked into his new therapist's office, he could feel his heart beating in his throat. His hands were clamming up, and his anxiety was practically screaming at him to turn around and go back home — but he stayed. It took a minute for him to warm up to his therapist, but once he started talking about his thoughts and feelings, he realized that she wasn't there to judge him. She was actually listening to what he was saying, and trying to understand.

After just a few weeks of attending therapy, Charles began to feel better. His therapist told him about some coping strategies he could use to deal with his anxiety while at work or social gatherings. He learned that he wasn't alone in his struggles with anxiety and that seeking help is actually a sign of strength, not weakness. Of course, Charles's anxiety didn't disappear completely, but he had the tools to manage it now — which made him feel more safe and secure in all areas of his life.

He started talking to his girlfriend, friends, and family about his experiences with anxiety, and was surprised to find out that many of them struggled with anxiety as well. In the end, he was proud of himself for facing his anxiety head-on and getting the help he needed. He also hoped that his story would encourage other people in his position to seek help as well, which is why I've been sharing his story with you throughout this book.

In this chapter, we'll take a closer look at some of the main anxiety management strategies Charles learned about below. I encourage you to take some time to try out the techniques and exercises that speak to you —

especially if you're feeling anxious about an upcoming work presentation or social event. You might be surprised by how helpful the following anxiety management strategies can be. Who knows? Maybe you'll decide to integrate some of them into your daily routine. Let's dive right in, shall we?

RELAXATION TECHNIQUES

Have you ever had someone tell you to "just relax?" This can obviously be frustrating, especially for people with anxiety — who want, more than anything, to be able to relax! If you've ever experienced intense anxiety, you know that managing it isn't as simple as just relaxing. That's where relaxation techniques, like mindfulness meditation and progressive muscle relaxation, come in. These techniques are typically used in conjunction with other types of therapy, such as cognitive behavioral therapy and exposure therapy.

Relaxation techniques are meant to focus on the body and reduce anxiety symptoms like muscle tension. Practicing these techniques can help you slow down your breathing and heart rate, as well as quiet your racing thoughts. In addition to practicing these techniques, doing things you enjoy and spending time with the people you love most can also help you to feel more relaxed. Let's go over some of the best relaxation techniques I came across in my research below.

Progressive Muscle Relaxation

I briefly touched on progressive muscle relaxation in the last chapter, but I'd like to take this opportunity to really get into the nitty-gritty of this particular relaxation technique. Progressive Muscle relaxation helps to counteract your body's natural response to stress, which is known as the fight-or-flight response. This response is necessary, as it can help you respond in a way that protects you when you find yourself in a dangerous situation. However, people who suffer from anxiety often find that their fight-or-flight response gets triggered too often, and by things that aren't actually dangerous at all.

When your fight-or-flight response gets activated, it can put a lot of stress on your body. This is why anxiety sufferers will oftentimes experience physical symptoms — like stiffness and muscle pain. Relaxation techniques, like progressive muscle relaxation, essentially have the opposite effect on your body. Practicing progressive muscle relaxation is meant to trigger your body's relaxation response, which reduces your heart rate and alleviates any bodily tension. Progressive muscle relaxation can also help people become more aware of how their mental and physical stress is affecting them emotionally. This sense of awareness may eventually help you let go of the anxious thoughts and feelings that come up in stressful situations.

How to Practice Progressive Muscle Relaxation

In order to better understand how progressive muscle relaxation works, I recommend trying this quick exercise. Make a tight fist with one of your hands, and notice any tightness and tension in your fingers and forearm. Count to ten, then release your first and allow your hand to relax completely. You should notice a huge difference in tension, and feel much more relaxed than you did before.

This approach of systematically increasing and then releasing tension in different muscle groups throughout your body is the basis for progressive muscle relaxation. By creating tension in your body, noticing it, and then releasing that tension, you can effectively learn how to alleviate your stress and get rid of your anxious thoughts. If you'd like to practice some progressive muscle relaxation right now, I would suggest finding a comfortable place to sit or lie down where you won't get distracted. Feel free to close your eyes if that helps you relax, but it's not required for this exercise.

Start by taking three to five deep breaths. Make sure to inhale through your nose and exhale through your mouth. Tense up your feet and begin to work your way up your body, tensing and releasing each muscle group, including your legs, glutes, abdomen, back, hands, arms, shoulders, neck, and face. Hold each muscle group for a few breaths before slowly releasing the tension. I recommend repeating this process in any areas where you feel particularly tense. Finish up by taking a few more deep breaths, and take note of how much more relaxed you feel.

Keep in mind that progressive muscle relaxation takes practice, so don't be discouraged if you feel like it doesn't immediately get rid of your bodily tension. Nothing is instantaneous, especially when it comes to managing anxiety symptoms. Keep practicing every day, and you'll eventually see results. Remember to be patient with your mind and body! That's a big part of using relaxation techniques like this to cope with your anxiety.

Mindfulness Meditation

Chances are, you've heard about mindfulness meditation. Perhaps your boss leads you and your coworkers in a mindfulness meditation exercise at the start of every work day (in which case, you have an awesome boss), or maybe you had a professor in college who ended every class with a mindfulness meditation exercise. As the name suggests, mindfulness meditation combines meditation with mindfulness — which involves being fully present in the moment and acknowledging your thoughts and feelings without judgment.

Mindfulness meditation can be done in a lot of different ways, but it usually involves deep breathing and being aware of your mind and body. You don't need to use essential oils or candles while meditating unless you want to (some people find that these things help them relax). All you need is a quiet and comfortable place to sit for a few minutes. Remember: it's very important that you approach mindfulness meditation with a non-judgmental attitude.

How to Practice Mindfulness Meditation

At the beginning of your mindfulness meditation journey, you might find it difficult to sit quietly, especially if there are a lot of distracting things happening around you. This is actually a normal part of mindfulness practice. Again, mindfulness involves being aware of how sitting still can make your thoughts race — but not judging those thoughts. I recommend starting with short meditation sessions, and gradually increasing the duration of these sessions as you become more comfortable with the practice.

It's always a good idea to choose a quiet, distraction-free place to meditate. This might be a little difficult for people with pets or small children, but just do the best you can. Wear comfortable clothing and remove your jewelry, shoes, or anything else that could potentially distract you. The goal is to create a peaceful and comfortable environment. Feel free to use things like candles, calming music, and essential oils while you meditate, but again, these things aren't necessary.

Here's a 20-minute guided mindfulness meditation you can do when you're feeling especially anxious: To begin this mindfulness meditation practice, start with a quick check-in. This will help you to become more aware of your current mental and physical state. Once you've done this, slowly direct your attention to your breathing.

Next, recall a specific event where you experienced anxiety. Be mindful of how this experience made you feel. Don't judge the anxiety or try to push it away — just observe it as it is. Take note of any emotions that come up during this reflection. Keep in mind that if you don't experience strong emotions, it doesn't mean you're doing the meditation incorrectly. Everyone experiences different emotions while practicing mindfulness meditation, and there's no "right way" to feel during it.

As you become more mindful of your anxiety, it may bring forth deeper layers of memories, thoughts, feelings, and physical experiences. Allow yourself to observe these thoughts and feelings without judgment and simply notice them as they arise. When you're ready, you can gradually shift your focus back to your breathing. As you bring this meditation to a close, take a moment to congratulate yourself for practicing mindfulness and listening to your mind and body. Not a lot of people are able to take the initiative to check in with their anxiety, but getting into the practice of doing so is a huge step towards overcoming your anxiety issues.

YOGA

Sometimes, when people start to experience feelings of anxiety or are going through particularly stressful times, they turn to yoga for relief. The beauty of yoga is that it meets you where you're at. Even practicing one or two poses for just a few minutes every day can have a pretty significant impact on you're well-being if you're open to it. The combination of focusing on your breathing and being present during each yoga pose can help quiet your negative thoughts and improve your mood. Yoga is also really good for your body and can release a lot of physical stress and tension.

To get the most out of practicing yoga, you should try to be mindful of the sensations moving throughout your body as you move through each pose. Allow yourself to feel and experience any emotions that happen to come up, but don't judge or criticize yourself for feeling a certain way or experiencing a certain thought. Practicing yoga is all about connecting with your body and living in the present moment.

If you find that your thoughts start to scatter during a yoga session, don't worry. This happens all the time, and it's best not to judge yourself for it. Gently refocus your attention back on your mat, and continue moving through your poses. Try to keep in mind that yoga is a journey, and the more you practice, the easier it'll become for you to focus on the present moment as well as release any anxious thoughts or emotions that may be weighing you down. Let's go over some yoga poses that you can try out on your own below.

Yoga Poses

Yoga is a physical and spiritual practice that has been around for thousands of years. It's an excellent stress reliever, and it's been proven to improve flexibility and

146 | KIRK TEACHOUT

increase bodily strength as well. There are *a lot* of different yoga poses, and each one is uniquely beneficial in its own way. Listed below are a few poses you can try out if you're looking to not only reduce your anxiety symptoms but improve your health and well-being overall.

The Channel-Cleaning Breath (Nadhi Shodhana)

This is a breathing exercise that can help to calm down your mind and reduce your stress. It involves alternating nostrils while breathing in and out. Pretty simple, right? This practice is often done before starting a yoga session in order to help clear the mind and focus on the practice that's ahead.

The Hero Pose (Virasana)

The Hero pose is a seated pose that yoga experts say can help to improve circulation and digestion. It can also help to stretch out your ankles and your knees, so this might be a great pose for you to try out if you spend a lot of time sitting or standing.

The Tree Pose (Vrikshasana)

The Tree pose is a standing pose that can help to improve your balance and overall stability. It involves standing on one foot with the other foot placed on the thigh of whichever leg you're standing on. This pose can also help to strengthen your legs, hips, and core. This one may take some practice, so don't be discouraged if you fall over on your first try!

The Extended Triangle (Utthita Trikonasana)

You'll do this pose while standing as well. The Extended Triangle pose can help to strengthen your legs and core. It involves reaching one arm down to the ground while extending the other arm up toward the ceiling.

The Standing Forward Bend (Padangusthasana)

The Standing Forward Bend is a forward fold pose that can help you stretch out your hamstrings and lower back. It's an especially great pose for releasing tension and calming the mind, so I definitely recommend giving it a try.

The Cat and Cow Poses (or Marjaryasana and Bitilasana, Respectively)

These poses are quite similar, and they're often done together in order to warm up the spine and stretch out the neck, hips, and shoulders. Both of these poses involve alternating between arching your back and rounding it (much like a cat).

The Bridge Pose (Setubandha)

The Bridge pose is a backbend type of pose that can help to strengthen your hips, core, and legs. It can also help to stretch out your chest, shoulders, and neck. This one feels great, but it definitely takes some practice.

BREATHING EXERCISES

Most of the time, breathing is something you do without really thinking about it. It's just a natural part of being alive! Some people who suffer from severe anxiety, however, have to think a bit more about their breathing. A lot of the symptoms that are associated with anxiety can cause a person with an anxiety disorder to breathe in a way that can lead to all sorts of physical and emotional problems. Oftentimes, your breathing is actually what causes uncomfortable anxiety symptoms, such as shortness of breath, and the reason for that is that your anxiety and stress are not allowing you to breathe properly.

Thankfully, there are plenty of great breathing exercises out there that can help you to more effectively regulate your breathing and cope with your anxiety. The exercises discussed below will teach you how to slow down your breathing in times of stress. The especially great thing about these exercises is that you can do them whenever and wherever you need to. Let's dive right in, shall we?

Deep Breathing

Deep breathing is one of the most popular techniques people with anxiety use to calm down when they're feeling stressed out. It involves inhaling slowly and deeply, holding your breath for a few seconds, and then exhaling. Repeat this exercise several times until you're feeling nice and relaxed. This might take a few minutes, so be patient with yourself!

The Quieting Response

The Quieting Response technique is another breathing exercise that can help to reduce your stress and anxiety as it literally activates your body's relaxation response. It involves breathing in deeply through your nose and then exhaling slowly through your mouth while making a "shh" sound. This technique helps slow down your heart rate and relax your muscles. I can't recommend it enough!

Belly Breathing

Belly breathing (which is also known as diaphragmatic breathing) is an especially popular breathing exercise. It involves breathing deeply from your belly instead of from your chest. This technique has been proven to reduce stress by activating one's parasympathetic nervous system. To practice this exercise, place one hand on your belly and the other on your chest. From there, inhale slowly through your nose and exhale slowly through your mouth.

Pursed Lips Breathing

Pursed lips breathing is a technique that can help you regulate your breathing and cut down on anxiety symptoms like shortness of breath. It involves inhaling through your nose and then exhaling slowly through your pursed lips (as if you're whistling). This technique helps to slow down your breathing and relax your muscles, so if you have muscle tension, it's definitely worth a try.

GROUNDING TECHNIQUES

If you suffer from anxiety, you're undoubtedly familiar with the unpleasant physical symptoms that typically accompany an anxiety attack. Your heart rate increases, your mouth gets dry, and your body starts to shake. You might also experience cold sweats and a sense of panic that can be awfully overpowering despite it being irrational. People with anxiety disorders, such as PTSD, often become absorbed in thoughts of past traumas or future uncertainties, which can trigger their fight-or-flight response. As I've already discussed, this common response can make one's brain perceive something that's not threatening as threatening, which can cause your body to prepare for a potential attack.

Using grounding techniques is an excellent way to cope with anxiety attacks, so it's a shame they're not talked about more. Grounding techniques are techniques that can help distract you when you're dealing with anxiety or panic attack symptoms. These techniques can be physical or mental and they can help you focus on the present moment and your surroundings, rather than on your anxious thoughts. Basically, by using grounding techniques, you can significantly reduce the intensity of your fight-or-flight response and regain a sense of control over your body and mind. Let's take a look at some common grounding techniques below. I recommend using one or two of these techniques when you begin to feel a panic attack coming on.

Physical Grounding Techniques

One of the most popular grounding techniques out there is the 5-4-3-2-1 technique. This technique involves naming five things you can see, four things you can touch, three things you can hear, two things you can smell, and one thing you can taste in order to distract yourself during a moment of panic. By focusing on these sensory experiences, you can shift your attention away from your anxious thoughts and emotions, and become more grounded in the moment — which, of course, is what truly matters.

Another way to ground yourself is by using certain physical sensations to sort of "trick" yourself and divert your attention away from your anxiety symptoms. For example, you can pour water over your hands, clench your fists and then release them, or wrap a heated blanket around your body. By paying attention to these sensations, you'll be able to calm yourself down and feel more at ease.

Mental Grounding Techniques

Mental grounding techniques can also be quite helpful. For example, some people with anxiety will play memory games in their minds in order to distract themselves from their symptoms. Try to think in categories, use math and numbers, recite something, or make yourself laugh by reading a joke book or watching a funny video. These techniques can help shift your focus away from your anxiety and towards something a little healthier. You'll be able to give yourself a more structured and controlled mindset, and there's a lot of power in that.

SEGUE

Coping with anxiety isn't easy, but with a little time and practice, it's totally possible. Now that you have the right information and tools on hand, you should be able to effectively soothe yourself when you're feeling anxious or stressed out. In the next chapter, I'll start to wrap things up and discuss some daily habits you can integrate into your routine if you want to live a less anxious life.

8

DAILY HABITS FOR A LESS
ANXIOUS LIFE

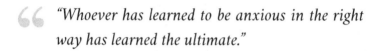 *"Whoever has learned to be anxious in the right way has learned the ultimate."*

— SØREN KIERKEGAARD

E very single one of us has habits — good and bad. Perhaps you've gotten into the habit of flossing daily, or maybe you chew your fingernails when you're feeling bored or stressed out. You've probably heard the phrase "old habits die hard." There's a lot of truth in that. It's *hard* to give up bad habits that you've been indulging in for a long time, but it's not impossible. The more you tell yourself that it's impossible, the harder it'll be to overcome anxious habits like isolating yourself from your friends or drinking too much as a way of coping with your anxiety.

When it comes to altering your habits and making lifestyle changes, it's important to start small. Although some bad habits — like smoking cigarettes — may be effectively overcome using the "cold turkey" method, social anxiety habits, such as refusing to go out with your friends, should be overcome by taking baby steps. It's easy for people with anxiety to get overstimulated when too much is happening at once. Most anxious people carry a heavy fear of change around with them, which is why plunging yourself into the icy water might not be the best way to go about altering your lifestyle. Take your time, and inch yourself in. Eventually, you won't even notice how cold the water is.

Take this quote from Linda Esposito on Psychology Today: "You can read all the anti-anxiety advice in the world, but none of it matters unless you take action. To feel more relaxed, to sleep soundly at night, and to put energy into what matters, you have to stop wasting time on tasks that don't matter." In order to truly experience relief and achieve a more relaxed state of mind, you must take action and actively work towards reducing the stress and anxiety in your life. This might involve prioritizing tasks that are important to you and avoiding wasting time on activities that aren't actually benefiting you all that much.

By focusing on tasks that are meaningful and avoiding those that are not, you can channel your energy and attention toward the things that matter most. Keep in mind that you may need to set boundaries with certain people or give up activities that drain your energy if you want to change your lifestyle for the better. Soon enough, you'll be able to create a daily routine that supports your mental health and allows room for activities that truly bring you joy. Let's take a look at some anxiety-reducing habits that you can begin to integrate into your daily routine below. Follow these tips, and you'll be that much closer to taking your life back from anxiety.

GET SOME SLEEP

I know that this is definitely easier said than done for people with anxiety, but just bear with me. If your anxiety has been keeping you from getting a good night's sleep, your lack of sleep has likely been making your anxiety worse. It's a vicious cycle. You can't sleep *because* of your anxiety, and your anxiety acts up *because* you can't sleep. Don't worry, though, because there are a few things you can do to break this cycle and finally get some shut-eye.

What to Do When You Can't Sleep

One of the best things you can do is establish a consistent sleep routine. Try to go to bed at the same time every night and wake up at the same time every morning. Yes, this includes weekends! If you're having trouble falling asleep, try getting up and doing something relaxing — like taking a warm bath or watching an ASMR video — until you feel more sleepy. It may also be helpful to limit naps to less than an hour during the day.

You should also try to avoid caffeine (coffee, soda, etc), as caffeine can take up to eight hours to wear off. If you have panic attacks, it might be a good idea to avoid caffeine entirely. You should also review your medications with your doctor to see if any of your daily stimulants have been keeping you up at night.

Creating a comfortable sleep environment is also crucial. Keep your bedroom cool, dark, and quiet, and avoid using electronic devices like your phone or computer while in bed (unless you're listening to relaxing music or watching a relaxing video to help you sleep). If your mattress is uncomfortable, consider buying a new one. It'll be well worth the investment! If you're still having trouble falling asleep, try meditating or practicing deep breathing. Keep a sleep log to track your sleep patterns and monitor your progress. This will be a good way to determine whether or not the methods you've been trying are helping or not.

WATCH WHAT YOU EAT

Did you know that maintaining a healthy diet is a crucial part of effectively managing anxiety? As delicious and comforting as pizza and soda may be, chances are, these unhealthy foods are negatively affecting your mental health. When it comes to eating healthy, there are a lot of dietary factors to consider. You should be hydrating properly, and getting enough complex carbohydrates (typically found in fruits and vegetables). It's also a good idea to avoid foods that are high in simple carbohydrates and to eat regularly to prevent your blood sugar from dropping too low.

Anti-Anxiety Foods

Nobody is born knowing what to eat when it comes to maintaining a healthy diet and quelling anxiety symptoms. Listed below are some foods you should keep in mind the next time you take a trip to your local grocery store or farmer's market:

- Fatty fish
- Eggs
- Probiotics
- Pumpkin seeds
- Yogurt
- Green tea
- Asparagus
- Dark chocolate
- Turmeric
- Chamomile
- Brazil nuts
- Magnesium
- Antioxidant-rich foods (such as black beans, cherries, blueberries, apples, nuts, and leafy greens)
- Zinc
- Vitamin B

EXERCISE

If you've ever felt less stressed out after going for a run or working out with your friends at the gym, there's a good reason for it. To quote Elle Woods from *Legally Blonde* (2001): "Exercise gives you endorphins. Endorphins make you happy! Happy people don't shoot their husbands. They just don't!" Basically, when you take care of your body, you are taking care of your mind as well. It can be difficult to get into a daily exercise routine at first, but take it as slowly as you need to. Even just going for a nature walk for thirty minutes every other day is better than nothing.

DETOX FROM SOCIAL MEDIA

If you're like most people, your relationship with social media has become a daily habit, and — whether you're aware of it or not — social media absolutely consumes your mental energy. We're constantly checking our phones for notifications, taking pictures for Instagram, and engaging in heated debates on Twitter and Facebook. Although social media can be fun, it's frankly gotten a little bit out of control. Thankfully, for people with anxiety, a social media detox can offer some much-needed relief.

It's important to remember that social media is not an accurate representation of real life. It presents a curated and selective view of the world, and people are beginning to recognize this fact. Consequently, there has been a growing trend of people reducing their social media usage, with some even deleting their accounts altogether. Social media, however, can be a harrowing addiction. While some people are able to quit cold turkey, many will quit for a short period of time and then go back to it. I think this is actually okay, though. Sometimes, people just need a break.

You don't need to go to extreme measures in order to reap the benefits of a social media detox. Simply taking a break from social media can help alleviate the anxiety that's associated with excessive social media use. So, instead of reaching for your phone first thing in the morning, I recommend trying to use your mental energy for more productive purposes. Go for a walk in nature, or curl up with your favorite book and a cup of coffee. By taking a step back from social media, you should be able to redirect your focus to the things that are truly important to you in life.

TREAT YOURSELF AND PRACTICE SELF-CARE

When you think about self-care, your mind might conjure up images of luxurious face masks, soothing massages, or an indulgent bubble bath with a glass of wine in hand. However, let's not forget that self-care doesn't have to be expensive or involve excessive pampering. In fact, some of the most impactful self-care practices are completely free and can transform your life if you learn how to integrate them into your daily routine. Self-care is a versatile term. It basically encompasses any sort of action we take that prioritizes our physical and mental health. This means that while we may associate self-care with spoiling ourselves, it's really just about taking care of ourselves in small and meaningful ways.

Things You Can Do to Treat Yourself

Simple activities — such as stretching and dancing around the living room — can improve your mood and help you get into a more relaxed state of mind. Movement, in general, is a great way to release all of that tension and stress that's been building up over time. Doing little things for yourself, like making your bed in the morning or planning your dream vacation, can give you a boost of energy, as can practicing positive self-talk in the mirror or going for a walk in the park.

If you often feel stressed about things like work and house chores, writing an "it's done" list could be a great way to keep track of everything you have to do. It'll also make you feel more productive and accomplished, which is always nice. Taking short naps throughout the day or engaging in mindfulness meditation exercises are also excellent ways to practice self-care. I also recommend journaling fairly regularly, as that can be a great way to keep track of your thoughts as well as the progress you've been making with overcoming your anxiety.

Remember to celebrate the little things. Make a special dinner for your significant other when the weekend finally rolls around, or treat yourself by doing absolutely nothing after you get home from work. You can also practice self-care while you're at work by taking frequent breaks, chatting with your coworkers, and going for little walks around the block every now and then. Do things that make you happy every single day, and your anxiety symptoms will lessen. It may take some time, but it will absolutely be worth it.

DECLUTTER

Life tends to build up, and sometimes, there's just way too much going on in your personal space. Clutter can be overwhelming for people with anxiety, so it's a good idea to declutter your space every once in a while. That said, it's important that you take it slow and start small. Begin by choosing just one small area in your home to organize — like a drawer or a shelf — and work on that until it's completely decluttered. The last thing you want to do is overwhelm yourself further by attempting to declutter everything at once.

Once you've cleared out the clutter from the space you're working on, consider categorizing your belongings into four different boxes, which you can mark "keep," "donate," "toss," or "sell." This should make the decluttering process a whole lot easier for you, and hey — it's a good excuse to have a yard sale.

Try to keep in mind that decluttering isn't a one-time event. It's an ongoing process, and it's certainly more of a marathon than it is a sprint. Decluttering can also extend beyond your physical things. Consider making your office space paperless, adding a "no junk mail" sign to your letterbox, and keeping track of the clothing you typically wear. These small changes can help you create a more minimalist, stress-free environment for yourself.

SEGUE

Changing your lifestyle can be challenging, but if you're willing to take baby steps, you should eventually be able to alter your bad habits and reduce your anxiety. Getting more exercise, watching what you eat, and engaging in daily self-care activities are all excellent ways to quell your anxiety symptoms. Figure out what works best for you and keep at it. Although it might take a little bit of time, you're bound to see some significant improvements.

CONCLUSION

Anxiety is one of the most commonly experienced mental illnesses in the world. It's honestly baffling that people don't talk about it more! The more you're able to understand your anxiety, the more success you'll have in eventually overcoming it (or, at the very least, learning how to manage it effectively). When it comes to coping with and overcoming your anxiety symptoms, one of the first things you're going to want to do is identify your triggers.

Some of the most common anxiety triggers include money problems, grief, illness, and job loss or work stress. In essence, big life changes can be difficult for people with anxiety to grapple with, as can significant past trauma — such as events that caused you emotional pain during your childhood or bad experiences you've had in past romantic relationships. Social anxiety can also be a huge problem, as it can negatively affect your relationships with your loved ones and prevent you from living your best life.

Thankfully, there are a whole lot of strategies and methods you can use to cope with your anxiety these days. Practicing things like mindfulness meditation and progressive muscle relaxation can have a significant impact on your mind and body, as well as reduce your anxiety symptoms (as long as you're willing to stick with it and practice every day). Some people with anxiety choose to take up yoga, which can really help with physical symptoms like muscle tension and stiffness. Practicing breathing exercises and engaging in grounding techniques can also help those who are experiencing a lot of anxiety all at once. These things tend to be especially helpful in the context of panic attacks.

By taking the actions required to slowly alter your habits, you can eventually change your life for the better. Getting daily exercise and keeping better track of what you eat can work wonders, as can getting more sleep and practicing self-care. Most people don't do enough things that bring them genuine joy in their daily lives, which is just one reason why anxiety is on the rise. It took my friend, Charles, a long time to learn this. However, when things clicked for him, he knew exactly how to take control of his anxiety and change his life.

Now that you have a lot more tools and information on hand, you should be able to take that first step toward overcoming your anxiety. I believe in you! As I mentioned before, this process won't be easy, but you'll be glad that you put the time and effort into taming the beast that's been holding you back from experiencing all of the joys life has to offer. Charles (and many others) eventually learned how to tame the beast with many faces, and you can too!

I hope that this book taught you something new, and helped you understand the complex nature of anxiety in a new light. Living with anxiety is *hard*, but you'll get through this — especially since you have a brand new tool belt. Keep building up your support system, and don't be afraid to seek professional help for your anxiety if you find yourself continuing to struggle with it. If you want to help other people who are struggling with anxiety, you can do so by leaving a review. Reviews from people like you are what will make this book more visible to those who are seeking help and solace while dealing with this common affliction.

You did it!

I would like to take a moment to express my deepest gratitude to you for taking the time to read this book on overcoming anxiety. I know that there are many books out there on this topic, and I am honored that you chose mine. I hope that you have found value in the pages of this book and that it has provided you with practical strategies and tools to manage your anxiety.

Writing this book was a labor of love, and it is my sincere hope that it has made a positive impact on your life. I know firsthand how challenging anxiety can be, and I wrote this book with the hope of helping others who are struggling with similar challenges. Whether you are dealing with everyday worries or more severe anxiety, my goal was to provide you with a roadmap for managing your anxiety and living a more fulfilling life.

As I bring this book to a close, I would like to ask for your help. If you found value in this book, **please consider leaving an honest review on Amazon**. Your feedback is invaluable and will help others who are considering purchasing this book. Your review will also let me know how I can improve future editions, and I am always open to feedback and suggestions.

Once again, thank you for reading this book on overcoming anxiety. Your support and encouragement mean the world to me, and I hope that this book has provided you with the tools you need to manage your anxiety and live a more fulfilling life.

Your Friend,

Kirk Teachout

RESOURCES

10 easy ways to declutter your home: AIG Insurance Ireland. aig. (n.d.). Retrieved April 13, 2023, from https://www.aig.ie/our-blog/ways-to-declutter-your-home

9 common myths & facts about anxiety: Symptoms and treatment options. The Recovery Village Drug and Alcohol Rehab. (2022, May 26). Retrieved April 13, 2023, from https://www.therecoveryvillage.com/mental-health/anxiety/anxiety-myths/

American Psychological Association. (n.d.). *Anxiety*. American Psychological Association. Retrieved April 13, 2023, from https://www.apa.org/topics/anxiety

Anxiety disorders: Types, causes, symptoms & treatments. Cleveland Clinic. (n.d.). Retrieved April 13, 2023, from https://my.clevelandclinic.org/health/diseases/9536-anxiety-disorders

Association, A. C. M. H. (n.d.). *What's the difference between anxiety and an anxiety disorder?* What's the difference between anxiety and an anxiety disorder? | Here to Help. Retrieved April 13, 2023, from https://www.heretohelp.bc.ca/q-and-a/whats-the-difference-between-anxiety-and-an-anxiety-disorder

Cronkleton, E. (2018, June 6). *Yoga for anxiety: 11 poses to try, why it works, and more*. Healthline. Retrieved April 13, 2023, from https://www.healthline.com/health/anxiety/yoga-for-anxiety

Cuncic, A. (2020, May 30). *Seek help for the worst triggers in social anxiety*. Verywell Mind. Retrieved April 13, 2023, from https://www.verywellmind.com/which-situations-trigger-anxiety-3024887

Dan. (2021, October 20). *25 grounding techniques for anxiety*. Choose Mental Health. Retrieved April 13, 2023, from https://choosementalhealth.org/25-grounding-techniques-for-anxiety/

Dibdin, E. (2022, January 31). *When childhood trauma leads to anxiety*. Psych Central. Retrieved April 13, 2023, from https://psychcentral.

com/anxiety/the-connection-between-childhood-trauma-and-generalized-anxiety-disorder%23treatment-options

Exercise for stress and anxiety. Exercise for Stress and Anxiety | Anxiety and Depression Association of America, ADAA. (n.d.). Retrieved April 13, 2023, from https://adaa.org/living-with-anxiety/managing-anxiety/exercise-stress-and-anxiety

Forbes Magazine. (2023, March 9). *4 expert-backed breathing exercises for anxiety.* Forbes. Retrieved April 13, 2023, from https://www.forbes.com/health/mind/breathing-exercises-anxiety/

Grief and anxiety. Cruse Bereavement Support. (2021, November 15). Retrieved April 13, 2023, from https://www.cruse.org.uk/understanding-grief/effects-of-grief/grief-and-anxiety/

How anxiety affects men and women differently. How Anxiety Affects Men and Women Differently. (n.d.). Retrieved April 13, 2023, from https://www.texashealth.org/Health-and-Wellness/Behavioral-Health/How-Anxiety-Affects-Men-and-Women-Differently

Margarita Tartakovsky, M. S. (2017, November 20). *Why our family triggers USAND what to do.* Psych Central. Retrieved April 13, 2023, from https://psychcentral.com/blog/weightless/2017/11/why-our-family-triggers-us-and-what-to-do#1

Margarita Tartakovsky, M. S. (2021, September 14). *How to identify the real cause of your anxiety.* Psych Central. Retrieved April 13, 2023, from https://psychcentral.com/anxiety/getting-to-the-root-of-your-anxiety

Mayo Foundation for Medical Education and Research. (2020, March 11). *Obsessive-compulsive disorder (OCD).* Mayo Clinic. Retrieved April 13, 2023, from https://www.mayoclinic.org/diseases-conditions/obsessive-compulsive-disorder/symptoms-causes/syc-20354432

Mayo Foundation for Medical Education and Research. (2022, December 13). *Post-traumatic stress disorder (PTSD).* Mayo Clinic. Retrieved April 13, 2023, from https://www.mayoclinic.org/diseases-conditions/post-traumatic-stress-disorder/symptoms-causes/syc-20355967

Mcmaster, G. (2020, January 28). *Millennials and gen Z are more anxious than previous generations: Here's why.* Folio. Retrieved April 13, 2023, from https://www.ualberta.ca/folio/2020/01/millennials-and-gen-z-are-more-anxious-than-previous-generations-heres-why.html

MediLexicon International. (n.d.). *9 foods that help reduce anxiety.* Medical News Today. Retrieved April 13, 2023, from https://www.medicalnewstoday.com/articles/322652%23foods-that-help-reduce-anxiety

Melinda Smith, M. A. (2023, February 28). *Job loss and unemployment stress.* HelpGuide.org. Retrieved April 13, 2023, from https://www.helpguide.org/articles/stress/job-loss-and-unemployment-stress.htm

Migdol, E. (2023, February 28). *10 conditions that may be misdiagnosed as anxiety.* The Mighty. Retrieved April 13, 2023, from https://themighty.com/topic/chronic-illness/misdiagnosed-anxiety-symptoms/

Miller, H. A. (2020, July 14). *7 lesser known symptoms of anxiety.* Family Psychiatry & Therapy. Retrieved April 13, 2023, from https://familypsychnj.com/2020/07/7-lesser-known-symptoms-of-anxiety/

Murphy, A. (2022, July 4). *How to take a social media detox and improve your mental health.* Declutter The Mind. Retrieved April 13, 2023, from https://declutterthemind.com/blog/social-media-detox/

NHS. (n.d.). NHS choices. Retrieved April 13, 2023, from https://www.nhs.uk/mental-health/conditions/generalised-anxiety-disorder/symptoms/

Nicole J. LeBlanc, M. A., & Luana Marques, P. D. (2019, August 27). *Anxiety in college: What we know and how to Cope.* Harvard Health. Retrieved April 13, 2023, from https://www.health.harvard.edu/blog/anxiety-in-college-what-we-know-and-how-to-cope-2019052816729

Postpartum anxiety: Causes, symptoms, diagnosis & treatment. Cleveland Clinic. (n.d.). Retrieved April 13, 2023, from https://my.clevelandclinic.org/health/diseases/22693-postpartum-anxiety

Robinson, L. (2023, February 25). *Coping with financial stress.* HelpGuide.org. Retrieved April 13, 2023, from https://www.helpguide.org/articles/stress/coping-with-financial-stress.htm

Robinson, L. (2023, March 4). *Coping with a life-threatening illness or serious health event.* HelpGuide.org. Retrieved April 13, 2023, from https://www.helpguide.org/articles/grief/coping-with-a-life-threatening-illness.htm

Social anxiety disorder. Social Anxiety Disorder | Anxiety and Depression Association of America, ADAA. (n.d.). Retrieved April 13, 2023, from https://adaa.org/understanding-anxiety/social-anxiety-disorder

Sussex Publishers. (n.d.). *Getting past the past jealousy.* Psychology Today. Retrieved April 13, 2023, from https://www.psychologytoday.com/us/blog/anxiety-files/201804/getting-past-the-past-jealousy

Team, T. H. E. (2021, October 11). *What causes anxiety? risk factors and more.* Healthline. Retrieved April 13, 2023, from https://www.healthline.com/health/anxiety-causes%23causes

Tips for beating anxiety to get a better night's sleep. Harvard Health. (2020, October 13). Retrieved April 13, 2023, from https://www.health.harvard.edu/mind-and-mood/tips-for-beating-anxiety-to-get-a-better-nights-sleep

Toussaint, L., Nguyen, Q. A., Roettger, C., Dixon, K., Offenbächer, M., Kohls, N., Hirsch, J., & Sirois, F. (2021, July 2). *Effectiveness of progressive muscle relaxation, deep breathing, and guided imagery in promoting psychological and physiological states of relaxation.* Evidence-based complementary and alternative medicine : eCAM. Retrieved April 13, 2023, from https://www.ncbi.nlm.nih.gov/pmc/articles/PMC8272667/

WebMD. (n.d.). *Workplace anxiety: Causes, symptoms, and treatment.* WebMD. Retrieved April 13, 2023, from https://www.webmd.com/anxiety-panic/features/workplace-anxiety

What are anxiety disorders? Psychiatry.org - What are Anxiety Disorders? (n.d.). Retrieved April 13, 2023, from https://www.psychiatry.org/patients-families/anxiety-disorders/what-are-anxiety-disorders

What lifestyle changes are recommended for anxiety and depression? Taking Charge of Your Health & Wellbeing. (n.d.). Retrieved April 13, 2023, from   https://www.takingcharge.csh.umn.edu/what-lifestyle-changes-are-recommended-anxiety-and-depression

Wolff, C. (2018, January 10). *21 quick, life-changing self-care hacks that don't cost you anything*. Bustle. Retrieved April 13, 2023, from https://www.bustle.com/p/21-quick-life-changing-self-care-hacks-that-dont-cost-you-anything-7842786

Printed in Great Britain
by Amazon

37084160R00099